A PORTRAIT OF THE

DOG

A PORTRAIT
OF THE
DOG

ANDREW MORRIS

FALL
RIVER

PRESS

Fall River Press
122 Fifth Avenue
New York, NY 10011

ISBN: 978-1-4351-0726-7

1 3 5 7 9 10 8 6 4 2

Printed in Singapore

CONTENTS

INTRODUCTION

Mankind's relationship with the dog can be traced back thousands of years. Indeed, the dog is probably our oldest non-human companion. Excavations of fossils in the Middle East, believed to be at least 12,000 years old, reveal a touching reminder of the enduring bond between man and dog, for on this site was found the skeleton of a dog lying next to the remains of its master.

Interestingly, for an animal that has been so important to us for so very long, there is uncertainty as to the exact way in which domestication of the dog occurred. We cannot even be absolutely sure of the evolutionary route by which the dog itself came about, although most experts are in agreement that the wolf is the most probable ancestor. Later, we shall look in more detail at the most likely theories as to how dogs evolved. We shall also explore some of the ways in which the dog may have begun to befriend human beings all those years ago.

A Portrait of the Dog does not include every breed in existence today, but those that are featured celebrate the dog's strength, beauty and usefulness to man in all its many forms.

CHAPTER ONE
HOUNDS

The common feature of all the dogs in this group is that they pursue game. If necessary, they then prevent the quarry from escaping, and may bark to pinpoint its location for the hunter before he arrives to dispatch it. Being able to corner the quarry in this way was a particularly important requisite before the advent of efficient guns.

Most of the dogs in this group are hounds that hunt by sniffing the ground to pick up and then follow a scent, calling and barking all the while. Dogs of this type include Foxhounds, Beagles and Bassets. The sport of hunting game on horseback – using a pack of hounds to track down the quarry – was a popular pastime in medieval France. There, kings and rich noblemen hunted in the extensive broad-leaved forests for fox, wild boar and deer. Later, following the Norman Conquest, the pursuit was introduced to England.

Keeping packs of hounds became a highly developed activity. Dogs were carefully bred to ensure continuity of the best strains for working over the terrain and to pursue a particular quarry. Furthermore, specific colors and types were selected in

ABOVE RIGHT: The Basset Hound may look mournful but it is an accommodating animal, as happy ambling through fields and sniffing out the terrain as it is idling away hours by the fireside.

OPPOSITE: The elegant Borzoi is the total opposite of the Basset Hound and may not be everyone's idea of the perfect pet.

order to produce a uniform appearance throughout the pack. Large hounds with great strength and stamina were used to accompany hunters on horseback, chiefly in pursuit of fox, deer and wild boar. In due course, smaller mutations and Basset-type hounds were developed; these were used by hunters following on foot to capture smaller game such as badgers, rabbits and hares, when the dogs would usually be sent underground to flush the animals out of their lairs. For such work, dogs with specific features would be obtained through

selective breeding. These features included shorter legs to enable them to tunnel underground, and powerful jaws for dealing with the quarry.

The ancestor of the pack hound is the Chien de Saint-Hubert. For many centuries it was bred in a monastery in the Ardennes region of Belgium, and until the 1780s the monks there were required to give six hounds each year to the king. Although pure specimens of the breed eventually ceased to be found in Belgium or France, in England it continued to flourish in the form of the Bloodhound, a breed that was believed to have been brought to England by William the Conqueror. Despite popular belief, the name 'bloodhound' does not indicate the hound's ability to follow a blood trail – although its ability to smell out quarries is phenomenal – but refers to the fact that it is from pure bloodstock.

Some hounds hunt primarily by sight, one of the best-known of these sighthounds being the Greyhound, which relies on its eyes rather than its nose to detect prey before giving chase. Then, the dog uses its enormous speed and power to overtake and dispatch the quarry. In some countries of the Middle East hunters, mounted on horseback, take with them their sighthounds, which are released once a quarry is detected. Other typical sighthounds include Salukis, Whippets and Afghans – all characterized by their long-legged, supple and slender bodies that are capable of carrying the dogs at speed.

In Russia, during the time of the tsars, noblemen and royalty kept packs of fast-running hounds that were capable of bringing down wolves. Usually the wolves were pursued first by Greyhounds and other lightly built hounds before they were overcome by a second wave of stronger hounds such as Borzois.

There are some hounds that encompass the virtues both of the scenthounds and the sighthounds. They include the Pharaoh Hound and the Ibizan Hound, characterized by their sleek appearance and large, erect ears. Some of these breeds are of very ancient origin; similar-looking animals adorn artefacts found buried in the tombs of the Egyptian pharaohs thousands of years ago, proving that dogs such as these were prized by the rulers of these early civilizations.

Another group, the Spitzes, are multipurpose hounds. The group includes breeds such as the Elkhound and the Finnish Spitz. Typically, these dogs are large and stocky, with erect ears and bushy, tails curled over their backs, their thick coats helping them to keep warm in bitter weather. These large, tough dogs were bred to give chase to game such as wolves, elks and bears in frozen, wooded terrain and then to hold the game at bay, signaling their whereabouts with loud and distinctive calls. Today they are more commonly used for hunting gamebirds.

Many hounds, in addition to their skills as hunters and trackers, also make excellent guard dogs, and apart from a few breeds – such as Foxhounds, which are better suited to life as part of a hunting pack – members of the hound group invariably make friendly, gregarious, affectionate and loyal companions. Many, however, can become so absorbed by the work in hand that they tend, on occasions, to become a little deaf to the 'return' commands of their owners!

AFGHAN

As its name suggests, this ancient breed of sighthound (gazehound) originated in the rugged mountains and plains of Afghanistan. Despite its regal air and glamorous looks the Afghan is in fact a powerful hunter, and in its native land is used to guard and herd livestock. The first Afghans arrived in Britain in the early 1900s, the breed achieving great acclaim at the 1907 Crystal Palace show in London. Afghans were first imported into the USA in 1926.

Appearance Large and dignified while at the same time giving the impression of having great power and speed. The head is held proudly, the skull being long but not too narrow. The nose is black, although liver is permissible in dogs with lighter-colored coats. Dark eyes are preferred, but golden eyes can also occur. The almond-shaped eyes slant slightly upward at the outer corners. The ears are carried close to the head and are covered with long, silky hair. The well-muscled, moderate-length body, with its deep chest, is offset by long, strongly boned legs and a long tail with a ring at its tip.

Coat Long and fine, except on the foreface, and with a silky 'topknot.' Owners may find grooming the dog something of a task. Both fore and hind feet should be covered with long fur. All colors are acceptable.

Size *Height:* 25–29in (63.5–74cm). *Weight:* male 60lb (27kg); female 50lb (23kg).

The Afghan's original native name, the Tazi, betrays its connection with the very similar Tasy breed of Russia, the proximity of southern Russia with Afghanistan suggesting a common origin for both breeds.

Characteristics and Temperament

The distinctive high-stepping gait and long, flowing coat are characteristics of this breed. Intelligent, and with a distinctly oriental appearance, Afghans may also seem to be reserved and aloof, but they are quite capable of playing the fool when the mood takes them. They are also affectionate toward their owners, although they are one of the more demanding breeds to maintain and are not for the faint-hearted. Keepers of Afghans soon realize that this is a dog that owns them and not the other way around.

The reason a dog has so many friends is that he wags his tail instead of his tongue.

Anonymous

BASENJI

The Basenji has its origins in what is now the Democratic Republic of Congo, although dogs of similar are found throughout central Africa and may even be the palace dogs depicted at the time of the Egyptian pharaohs. In its native land, the

Also known as the Congo Dog, the Basenji was refined by British breeders and subsequently exported all over the world. In Africa, the dog is used to warn of the approach of dangerous animals, and as an active hunter of small game.

Basenji is still used as a guard dog, companion and hunter, being adept at catching small game and rodents. The first two examples were brought to Britain in 1895, but it was not until 1937 that imports were successfully bred in Britain. Basenjis were officially accepted by the American Kennel Club in 1943, and in 1990, the AKC stud book was reopened to several new imports at the request of the Basenji Club of America. Basenjis are also registered with the UK Kennel Club.

Appearance A fine-boned and lightly built animal, the Basenji always looks poised,

aristocratic and alert. The handsome head, with its wrinkled forehead, narrows toward the point of the nose, which should be black. The dark, almond-shaped eyes have a fixed, somewhat inscrutable expression. The ears are small, pointed and pricked. The neck is well-arched, long and strong. The body is short and deep, with a level back. The tail curls tightly over the back and lies to one side of the thigh in a single or double curl.

Coat Short, smooth and fine and recognized in the following standard colorations: red, black, tricolor (black with tan in the traditional pattern), and brindle (black stripes on a background of red), all with white.

Size *Height:* male 17in (43cm); female 16in (41cm). *Weight:* male 24lb (11g); female 21lb (9.5kg).

Characteristics and Temperament

Renowned for its cleanliness and lack of odor, the Basenji is an ideal pet, and being intelligent and curious the dog soon becomes bonded with its family. Basenjis do not bark; instead, they make unusual yodeling sounds when trying to express

themselves. Basenjis love to chew, even when past the puppy stage, so it is a wise precaution to provide plenty of toys for them to destroy.

BASSET FAUVE DE BRETAGNE

This little dog originally came from Brittany, France, where it was developed as a hunting dog from the larger Grand Fauve de Bretagne, now extinct. It was rumored, though probably untrue, that the Basset Fauve de Bretagne was near extinction after the Second World War, and that it was recreated using remaining examples of the breed crossed with the Petit Basset Griffon Vendéen and standard wirehaired Dachshunds. The middle breed, the Griffon Fauve de Bretagne, still exists but is far rarer than the Basset Fauve.

Appearance Notable in the Basset Fauve are the slightly aquiline, medium-length foreface and ears that are at the same level

as the eyes. The ears, with their distinctive pleat from root to point, are covered with finer, smooth hair and are of a darker color than the coat. The body has a wide, broad chest and slightly barrel ribs. The topline is level and the tail is carried in a sickle-like shape when on the move. Front legs are straight and the hindquarters are strong, typical of a working hound.

Coat Harsh and dense. Colors are golden-wheaten, red-wheaten, or fawn. A white spot on the chest is permitted.

Size *Height:* 12.5–15in (32–38cm). *Weight:* 35–40lb (16–18kg).

Characteristics and Temperament
Lively, friendly and not too big even for a small home, this dog is gaining popularity as a house pet. It is easy to groom and feed.

It should be remembered that the Basset Fauve is an active hound with a strong urge to hunt which owners should respect.

BASSET

The ancestor of the Basset Hound was believed to have been bred for hunting rabbits by scent by French monks in medieval times. A close relative of the French Bassets, the breed was nevertheless developed separately in Britain through crossings with Bloodhounds. The Basset was introduced to shows in Britain in 1875. The AKC first recognized the breed in 1885, and in 1935, the Basset Hound Club of America was organized in the US. The current American standard for the breed was adopted in 1964.

Appearance A heavily-built, slow-moving dog with a comical, worried expression. The long, broad head is heavily domed and bears long, pendulous ears. There is loose skin around the head and muzzle. The nose is black, although it can be brown or liver in lighter-colored dogs. The eyes are brown or hazel, with the red coloration of the inner lower lids plainly visible. The low-slung body is long, with a broad, deep chest and arched loins. Short, heavy legs end in

massive feet. On the move, the long, tapering tail is held up and slightly curved.

Coat Short and smooth but not too fine. Usually black, white and tan, but any recognized hound color is acceptable.

Size *Height:* 13–15in (33–38cm). *Weight:* 70lb (32kg).

Characteristics and Temperament
Tenacious and full of endurance, this is a dog that loves to paddle through wet fields sniffing the ground, although it is equally at home idling the time away by the fireside with its family. The Basset Hound's deep-chested bark might suggest an unfriendly disposition, but this would be a false impression, for this amiable dog is good-natured and placid. On the move, the Basset usually proceeds at a steady, lumbering pace, although it can break into a run should the need arise. The name Basset derives from the French word *bas*, meaning 'low.'

The dewlap, seen as the loose, elastic skin around the neck, together with the trailing ears, help trap the scent of whatever the Basset happens to be tracking.

BEAGLE

The smallest of the pack hounds, the Beagle is an English breed used for hunting hares with human followers coming on behind it on foot. It has been in existence since at least the reign of Henry VIII of England, and is deservedly popular in many countries, including North America, Britain and France.

Appearance A bustling, active and enthusiastic dog of compact build. The head is medium-to-broad with a slightly domed skull. The nose should preferably be black. The ears hang down to the cheeks and are thin, fairly long and rounded. Eyes are brown or hazel with a friendly expression.

A man may smile and bid you hail
Yet wish you to the devil;
But when a good dog wags his tail,
You know he's on the level.

Anonymous

The medium-length neck is carried on a short, deep-chested body, the strongly boned, muscular legs ending in round feet. The tail is fairly long and carried high.

Beagles came to the US in the 1840s, but were imported strictly for hunting and were of variable quality. They were accepted as a breed by the AKC in 1884.

Coat Dense, short and waterproof. Any recognized hound color is acceptable apart from liver.

Size *Height:* 13–16in (33–41cm). *Weight:* 20lb (9kg).

Characteristics and Temperament
Ever ready for action, not only is the Beagle happy hunting in a pack, but it is also equally content simply to be a pampered family pet. Bold, lively and affectionate, the dog is also blessed with stamina and intelligence. The short coat is quick to wash and dry, after even the muddiest of romps, but once free of the leash the Beagle is liable to take off after a scent trail, seemingly deaf to its owner's calls.

BLOODHOUND

The origins of the Bloodhound can be traced to Belgium, where legend has it that the breed was used for hunting in the Ardennes region as long ago as the 7th century. The Bloodhound was introduced to England by William the Conqueror in 1066. The name 'bloodhound' has been incorrectly attributed to the dog's legendary ability to follow a blood trail. In fact, the name signifies 'bloodstock' – and is a reference to the Bloodhound's aristocratic breeding.

Appearance A huge hound with great presence. The long, narrow head has characteristic hanging folds of pendulous skin, giving a somewhat lugubrious expression to the face. Eyes are brown or hazel. The long ears fall in graceful folds and feel soft to the touch. A long, throaty

neck is carried on a short, deep-chested body, and long, muscular legs contribute to the dog's imposing stature. The long, thick tail is carried high when on the move.

Coat Smooth, short and waterproof. Colors are black-and-tan, liver (red)-and-tan, and solid red. Small areas of white are permitted on the tail-tip, chest and feet.

Size *Height:* male 26in (66cm); female 24in (61cm). *Weight:* male 110lb (50kg); female 100lb (45kg).

Characteristics and Temperament
Known throughout the world for its remarkable ability to follow scents and trails, the Bloodhound is a robust, powerful animal with a deep, gruff bark. It is also generally affectionate, good-natured and tolerant, but can also be reserved – even sensitive. Being so large, Bloodhounds can be willful unless handled correctly.

The Bloodhound (also known as the Chien St.-Hubert) has been bred specifically for tracking, and is consequently often used to find escaped prisoners or missing persons. This scenthound is famous for its ability to follow a scent trail hours or even days old over long distances.

BORZOI

An ancient Russian breed, packs of Borzoi were once kept by almost all Russian noblemen. The largest Borzois were used in pairs for bringing down wolves – as their original name 'Russian Wolfhound' suggests. The first Borzois seen in England were presented to Queen Alexandra by the Russian tsar.

Appearance A graceful, aristocratic dog whose body suggests great power and speed. The long, lean head has a slightly domed skull, the jaws are long and powerful, and the nose is large with a black nose-leather. Eyes are dark, conveying intelligence, and the ears are small and pointed. The neck is slightly arched and muscular. A Borzoi's body should be comparatively short, rising to an arch at the loins and with a deep chest. The long, narrow legs are strong and muscular. The long tail is well-feathered.

Coat Silky, flat, curly or wavy; the hair is much longer on the body, with feathering on legs, chest, hindquarters and tail. Any color is acceptable.

Size *Height:* male 29in (74cm); female 27in (68.5cm). *Weight:* male 75–105lb (34–48kg); female 60–90lb (27–41kg).

Characteristics and Temperament
Rather aloof and self-possessed, this is not by any means a typical pet dog. Indeed, some examples may be rather temperamental, and ownership of one should be considered carefully. The Borzoi expresses its affection for its owner but is distrustful of strangers. For such a large animal, however, the Borzoi does not have a huge appetite.

The Borzoi is elegance personified – graceful both in motion and repose. It was originally bred for wild game coursing on open terrain, relying on its sight rather than scent.

COONHOUND

In the 17th century, British colonists in America imported Foxhounds into the state of Virginia so that they could continue hunting, also Bloodhounds to be used as guards for the settlements. During the second half of the 18th century, with the aid of progeny from the early Foxhounds, who were found to be inadequate for hunting animals that did not go to ground, Bloodhounds were added to the mix, the intention being to make them more suitable for hunting opossums and raccoons, bobcats and even larger prey, such as cougars and bears, which made their escape into the trees. Now named Coonhounds, although the dogs could not follow their quarry up trees, they were able to mill about below them, indicating the quarry's position to the hunters that followed behind. Of the various Coonhounds that were developed, the most important is the Black-and-Tan.

Appearance A large, powerful and alert dog with obvious Bloodhound ancestry. The head has a long, moderate-to-broad skull and a long, broad muzzle. The eyes are dark brown or hazel. The ears are long, pendulous and folded. The fairly long neck is carried on a medium-length body with a deep chest. Long, well-boned legs terminate in short, powerful feet. The tail is long and held aloft when on the move.

Coat Short and dense. There are several individual breeds of Coonhound that include the Black-and-Tan Coonhound, the Bluetick Coonhound, the English Coonhound, the Plott Hound, the Redbone Coonhound (*left*), the Treeing Walker Coonhound (*above*).

Size *Height:* male 25in (63.5cm); female 24in (61cm). *Weight:* male 90lb (41kg); female 80lb (36kg).

Characteristics and Temperament Keen and ready for action, this is a dog bred to withstand the cold of winter as well as the heat of summer. Coonhounds are friendly by nature but can be aggressive when required.

Foxhounds and other hunting hounds were imported to America from England, Ireland, and France, making up the initial composition of the dogs that were later known as Virginia Hounds. Bloodhounds were then added to many Coonhound lines to enhance their ability to track indigenous species.

DACHSHUND

The word Dachshund means 'badger dog' and describes the purpose for which these tough little dogs were originally bred in their native Germany. Their short legs and powerful jaws make them ideally adapted for entering setts and taking on their quarry underground. In fact, only the larger varieties were used for hunting badgers; the smaller ones hunted stoats and weasels. Not only did Dachshunds vary in size, but a range of coat types was also developed, with both types available in each of the two sizes. Today, Dachshunds are popular show dogs as well as working dogs.

Appearance A long and low dog with a muscular body. The long, lean head has a narrow skull and a long, fine muzzle. The eyes are medium-sized, almond-shaped and colored dark reddish-brown to brown-black. The ears are broad and well-rounded and hang flat to the head. The neck is rather long and muscular. The long body with its deep chest and level back must be held sufficiently clear of the ground to allow free movement. Legs are short and strong. The tail is long.

Coat *Smoothhaired:* Short, glossy and dense. *Longhaired:* Soft and straight or slightly waved; abundant feathering on underside and behind legs. *Wirehaired:* Whole body, except for the chin, ears, jaws and eyebrows should be covered in short, straight, harsh hair. All colors are permissible.

Size *Weight:* large varieties 26lb (12kg); small varieties 10lb (4.5kg).

Characteristics and Temperament
Intelligent and lively, Dachshunds need a firm hand and careful training being inclined to disobedience. Despite their small size, they make admirable watchdogs and are fearless in the protection of their family and friends, to whom they are very loyal. The Dachschund will normally eat whatever is placed before it – or whatever it may secure by its own means – so its diet must be controlled.

Dachshunds come in three sizes: standard, miniature and kaninchen. Although the first two sizes are recognized almost universally, the third size (which means rabbit) is recognized only by non-English speaking bodies like the Fédération Cynologique Internationale (World Canine Federation).

DEERHOUND

One of the oldest of all British breeds, the impressive-looking Deerhound was developed in the Scottish Highlands, being possibly the descendant of the hounds that accompanied the Celts as they migrated westward across Europe during the Bronze Age. Formerly used to bring deer to bay, the ending of the clan system in Scotland, following the Battle of Culloden in 1746, also meant the virtual demise of the noble breed. However, a few enthusiasts were able to ensure its survival, and the Deerhound still commands admiration and respect wherever it is seen.

Appearance The overall impression is of a larger, heavier-boned, rough-coated Greyhound. The head is long with a broad skull, pointed muzzle and no stop. The dark eyes appear gentle in repose but keen when the dog is aroused. The ears are small

and folded back when at rest and the nose is black. The head is carried on a long, muscular neck and the long body has well-arched loins and a deep chest. The legs are long and strongly boned. The tail

is long and tapering and almost reaches to the ground.

Coat Shaggy and thick; hard to the touch. The preferred color is dark blue-gray, but darker or lighter grays, brindles and yellows, sandy-red or red-fawn also appear.

Size *Height:* male 30in (76cm); female 28in (71cm). *Weight:* male 100lb (45kg); female 80lb (36kg).

Characteristics and Temperament
Speed, power and endurance are all suggested by the breed's build, but this is allied to a calm and dignified demeanor. The Deerhound is a gentle and friendly animal, ready to play and eager to please; considering its size it is remarkably unobtrusive about the house.

Most people keep their Deerhounds as pets and companions, but showing is also popular, as is hare-coursing, and the fact that a proportion of these dogs have been specifically bred for this activity has had a positive effect in keeping the breed healthy.

ELKHOUND

An ancient Norwegian dog of the Spitz type, which was used for hunting game, particularly elk. The Elkhound was developed for working in intensely cold conditions and over rough terrain, so it comes as no surprise that it should be so strong and hardy. The Elkhound achieved its distinctive form without intervention by mankind, and is a magnificent example of natural evolution.

Appearance The head has a broad skull with a long, broad muzzle and a marked stop. The slightly oval eyes have a fearless, yet friendly, expression. The ears are erect and pricked. The powerful neck holds the head high. The short body has a deep chest

with well-sprung ribs, while moderately long, strongly-boned legs terminate in comparatively small, oval feet. The tail is held curled tightly over the back.

Coat A coarse, straight, waterproof outercoat with a dense, soft, woolly undercoat. Color can be various shades of gray with black tips to the outercoat, being lighter on the chest, stomach, legs and underside of the tail.

Size *Height:* male 20.5in (52cm); female 19.5in (49.5cm). *Weight:* male 50lb (23kg); female 43lb (20kg).

Characteristics and Temperament
Hardy, bold and intelligent, the Elkhound is also friendly and independent, being dignified and showing no signs of nervousness. The breed has a loud and distinctive bark and a hearty appetite.

The Elkhound is the national dog of Norway, where it has been used to hunt, guard, herd, and defend. Its innate courage possibly comes from the fact that a significant number of them were once used to hunt bear and other large game.

FINNISH SPITZ

The national dog of Finland, with a breed standard going back to at least 1812, the Finnish Spitz is one of several Spitz breeds. The dog was originally bred to track game, such as bear and elk, in Finnish woodlands and to keep them at bay, marking their position for the hunter by means of its piercing bark. Nowadays it is used mainly to track birds such as black grouse. The puppies bear a strong resemblance to fox cubs.

Appearance The head is fox-like, with a gradually tapering muzzle. The medium-large eyes are dark and the expression is lively and alert. The nose should be completely black. The pricked ears are small and sharply pointed. A muscular,

The Finnish Spitz is quick and light on its feet, stepping out briskly and trotting with a lively grace. It single-tracks as the speed increases, and moves at a gallop when the hunt is underway.

medium-length neck is carried on the deep, almost square, body. The strong legs terminate in round feet. The bushy tail is held typically Spitz-like, curled over the back.

Coat This is fairly long, with a short, dense undercoat which is shorter on the head and legs. Color is a reddish-brown or red-gold on the back, with lighter shades elsewhere.

Size *Height:* male 17–20in (43–51cm); female 15.5–18in (39.5–46cm). *Weight:* male 31–36lb (14–16kg); female 23–29lb (10–13kg).

Characteristics and Temperament
Eager, courageous and intelligent, the Finnish Spitz is also lively and friendly. A good family pet but one that likes plenty of exercise; it is a rather vocal dog.

FOXHOUND

These are handsome dogs whose sole purpose is to hunt – usually as part of a pack. They are followed by huntsmen, usually on horseback, and will cover miles in search of their target. As a result, the breed is seldom seen in the show ring and is not generally regarded as a potential household pet. Intense selection and careful breeding, free from the influences of fashion, have kept the Foxhound at the peak of perfection.

Appearance A well-balanced dog with a rather broad, medium-length skull and a fairly long muzzle. The medium-sized hazel or brown eyes give the dog a keen expression. The broad, moderately long ears hang down flat. The neck is long and lean, and the body short and deep-chested. Long, well-boned legs terminate in round feet. The tail is long and held high.

Coat Short, dense and waterproof. Any hound color is permissible, including combinations of black, tan and white.

Size *Height:* 23–25in (58.5–63.5cm). *Weight:* 67lb (30kg).

Characteristics and Temperament
The Foxhound is a dog with plenty of stamina and endurance and with a natural

The first mention of Foxhounds being imported to America dates to 1650, when Robert Brooke sailed for the Crown Colony in America with a pack of hounds, which were to be the basis of several strains of American hounds. Hounds from France and England were brought in to further develop the breed in the middle to late 1700s.

hunting ability. Like all scenthounds, its sense of smell is extremely well-developed. The breed is also friendly and non-aggressive, while at the same time being somewhat determined and self-willed. With training, the breed can be kept as a house dog, but will need considerable exercise and feeding to make it feel at home.

GREYHOUND

Many experts believe the Greyhound had its origins in the Middle East, in that drawings of dogs resembling them have been found on the walls of ancient Egyptian tombs dating back to 4000 BC. The first of the so-called sighthounds or gazehounds, the breed was eventually developed to today's standard in Britain, the racing Greyhound being slightly smaller than the show dog. Greyhounds have been measured racing at speeds of over 45mph (72kph), making them some of the fastest of all the animals.

Appearance A strongly-built, muscular and symmetrical dog. The head is long with a broad skull and a long, strong muzzle. The dark eyes give it an intelligent expression. The ears are small and rose-shaped. The neck is long and muscular, while a deep and capacious chest allows plenty of space for heartand lungs. The back is long with powerful muscles, and there are slightly arched loins. Long, strongly-boned legs terminate in long feet. The tail is long.

Coat The fine coat lies close to the body. Colors may be black, white, red, fawn, brindle or fallow, or any combination of these colors with white.

Size *Height:* male 28–30in (71–76cm); female 27–28in (68.5–71cm). *Weight:* 60–70lb (27–32kg).

Despite their reputation, Greyhounds are not high-energy dogs. They are sprinters rather than endurance runners, and although they love to run they do not require extensive exercise. As pets, a brisk daily walk of as little as 20–30 minutes is all that is required.

Characteristics and Temperament
Greyhounds possess remarkable endurance and stamina together with a turn of speed that is second to none in the canine world. This is facilitated by the animal's long-reaching stride that swiftly covers the ground. Greyhounds are quiet, calm and affectionate dogs, even though they have a natural inclination to chase other, smaller animals. Nevertheless, they make good companions and pets.

*I would rather see the portrait of a dog that
I know, than all the allegorical paintings
they can show me in the world.*

Samuel Johnson

IBIZAN HOUND

A carved dish was found in the tomb of the Pharaoh Hemako bearing what appeared to be an image of an Ibizan Hound. The dish was made during Egypt's 1st Dynasty, thus indicating that the dog may have been a contemporary and favorite of the pharaohs, and other such tomb-paintings also bear this out. The breed takes its name from the Balearic island of Ibiza, and was probably taken there by Phenician traders, where it has been known, also on the nearby island of Formentera, for thousands of years. The Ibizan Hound is used for hunting hares, partridge and other game, either singly or as a member of a pack.

Appearance A finely-built dog with upright ears. The head has a long, narrow skull and muzzle. The nose is flesh-colored. Eyes are amber and fairly small, while the ears are large and pricked. A long, lean neck is carried on a body with a long, flat ribcage and arched loins. The legs are long and strong and terminate in hare-like feet. The tail is long and thin.

Coat The coat may be smooth or rough but always dense and hard, being longer beneath the tail. It can be white, 'lion'-colored, or any combination of the two.

Size *Height:* 22–29in (56–74cm). *Weight:* male 49lb (22kg); female 42lb (19kg).

Characteristics and Temperament
A renowned jumper, the breed needs plenty of space in which to exercise. Although they can be somewhat independent and stubborn, they nevertheless take well to training, as long as positive rather than punitive methods are used.

Lithe and racy, the Ibizan possesses a deer-like elegance combined with the power of a hunter. This is a hound of moderation, and with the exception of the ears should not appear extreme or exaggerated.

IRISH WOLFHOUND

No other dog attracts such admiring glances as the Irish Wolfhound. This magnificent breed was known to the Romans, and was held in great esteem from the 12th to the 16th centuries in Ireland, where it was used to hunt wolf, bear, stag and elk. When the last wolf became extinct in Ireland, the Wolfhound almost disappeared as well, but the breed was fortunately revived, using the few remaining specimens, in the mid-19th century. There is now a healthy and enthusiastic following for these animals – the tallest of any of the breeds of dog.

Appearance Of commanding size and appearance, coupled with muscular strength. The head is long, and the skull not too broad. The muzzle is long and moderately pointed. The nose is black, and the eyes are dark. The ears have a fine, velvety texture. The neck is long and muscular. A long body with a very deep chest and arched loins is carried on long, well-boned legs. The tail is long and slightly curved.

Coat Rough, hard and shaggy; long and wiry over the eyes and under the jaw. Colors are black, gray, red, brindle, fawn, wheaten, steel-gray or pure white.

Size *Height:* male 31in (79cm); female 28in (71cm). *Weight:* male 120lb (54kg); female 90lb (41kg).

Characteristics and Temperament
The breed's comparative rarity and huge size, together with its air of quiet dignity, set it apart from other dogs. Despite being such a large animal, the breed is renowned for its calm and friendly nature. It is also tolerant of children and obedient, which is necessary in so massive a creature.

In AD 1210 an Irish hound was send as a gift to Llewellyn, Prince of North Wales, by Prince John, later to be King John of England. This hound was probably the legendary Gelert, which was slain by Llewellyn in the mistaken belief that the hound had killed his baby son. In fact, the dog was covered with blood because it had recently killed a wolf that had found its way into the child's room.

There are only an estimated 1,000 or so Otterhounds in the world and somewhere between 350 and 400 in the United States. Moreover, they are now considered to be the most endangered dog breed in Britain, possibly making them more vulnerable even than the Giant Panda.

convey an amiable expression. The ears are long and pendulous. A long and powerful neck is carried on a strong, deep-chested body. Moderately long legs terminate in large and rounded webbed feet. The tail is thick at the base and tapers to a point.

Coat A dense, harsh and waterproof double coat. The fur on the head and lower legs is softer. A slightly oily feel may be apparent on the coat. All recognized hound colors are permitted.

Size *Height:* male 27in (68.5cm); female 24in (61cm). *Weight:* male 75–115lb (34–52kg); female 65–100lb (29–45kg).

OTTERHOUND

With an ancestry that includes French mixed with various strains of English hounds, the Otterhound is a long-established breed, and a pack of Otterhounds was known to have been kept by the English King John in 1212. When in 1977 the hunting of otters was banned in England and Wales, the breed declined. However, a campaign to have it recognized in Britain for showing purposes helped to restore its fortunes.

Appearance A large, rugged-looking dog, the head is heavy with a medium-to-broad skull and a deep muzzle. The head is impressive. The eyes are brown and help to

Characteristics and Temperament
The Otterhound was developed to spend much of its time hunting in water, but the breed can also travel long distances across rough country without tiring. A loud, baying bark and a keen nose for a scent are other features of this breed, which is also good-natured, intelligent and friendly. They are not the most stylish-looking dog by any means, but the Otterhound makes up for this by having such an engaging and endearing personality.

35

PETIT BASSET GRIFFON VENDÉEN

A breed that originated in France, the word 'basset' indicates a dog that is low to the ground, and as a scenthound it is used by sportsmen for trailing and beating game from cover. Introduced into Britain in 1969, this is still a comparatively rare dog.

Appearance A compact, short-legged hound. The head, carried on a long, strong neck, has a medium-length skull. The nose is black, and the large, dark eyes convey an intelligent and friendly expression. The supple ears end in oval shapes and are covered with long, fine hair. The medium-length body has a deep chest and is carried on stout, well-boned legs. The tail is of medium length and is carried proudly.

Coat Rough and long with a thick undercoat. Color is white with any combination of orange, lemon, tricolor or grizzle.

THIS PAGE: In the Vendée region of France, the Petit Basset Griffon is used to track rabbits and flush them out from their hiding-places, allowing the hunter to take the rabbits with a shot.

OPPOSITE: The Pharaoh Hound is the national dog of Malta, where it is called Kelb-tal-Fenek, meaning 'rabbit-hound.'

Size *Height:* male 13–15in (33–38cm); female 14in (35.5cm). *Weight:* male 42lb (19kg); female 39.5lb (18kg).

Characteristics and Temperament
Like most hounds, this dog is at its happiest when out in the countryside sniffing out trails. The dog's expression exemplifies its character – extrovert, happy and alert.

PHARAOH HOUND

For many years, the Pharaoh Hound was thought to be one of the oldest breeds, in that it resembled images of dogs featured on the walls of ancient Egyptian pyramids and tombs (*see also Ibizan Hound*). Recent DNA analysis, however, reveals that the breed is of a more recent date, having developed out of different lines of European hunting dogs. It is now indigenous to Malta and Gozo and remains rare outside of these islands.

Appearance A graceful-looking dog with a noble bearing. The head has a long skull and a long muzzle with a slight stop. The small, amber-colored eyes are oval and convey its intelligence. The ears are pricked.

A long, lean and strong neck is carried on a long body with a deep chest. The legs are also long and well-boned. The long tail is held high and curved when on the move.

Coat Fine or slightly harsh; short and glossy with no feathering. The basic color is a rich tan, sometimes with a white tail-tip, white mark on the chest, and white toes. A slim white blaze down the center of the face is also acceptable.

Size *Height:* male 22–25in (56–63.5cm); female 21–24in (53–61cm). *Weight:* 40–60lb (18–27kg).

Characteristics and Temperament
An alert hunter that tracks its prey by both scent and sight, this is a true working hound. But at the same time the Pharaoh Hound is friendly and affectionate, and is always in the mood to play. The short coat indicates that the dog should not be exposed to very cold conditions without protection.

RHODESIAN RIDGEBACK

The breed was developed by crossing native hunting dogs with others that were brought to southern Africa by Dutch farmers (Boers), who first emigrated from Europe in the 18th century. This eventually produced a larger dog that was ideal for hunting game and also for guarding property. The original native dogs had ridges on their backs, a feature that is now a characteristic of the Rhodesian Ridgeback. The dog, also sometimes called the African Lion Dog, was introduced to Rhodesia (now Zimbabwe) in the 1870s, where it was bred there in large numbers and eventually named for that country.

The hallmark of this breed is the ridge on the back that is formed by the hair growing in an opposite direction to the rest of the coat. The ridge should be clearly defined, and start immediately behind the shoulders and continue to a point between the prominence of the hips. It should contain two identical crowns (whorls) directly opposite one another. The lower edge of the crowns should not extend further than one third of the way down the ridge.

Appearance The head has a broad skull with a long, deep muzzle. The nose is black or brown. The eyes are round and bright and should tone with the coat-

color. The medium-sized ears are pendulous. The muscular body is fairly long and supports a long, strong neck. Legs are strong and muscular. The tail has a slight upward curve but is never curled.

Coat Short and dense, with a glossy, sleek appearance; the ridge of hair on the back should be clearly defined, tapering and symmetrical. Coat-color is light wheaten to red wheaten, with only small amounts of white permitted on the chest and toes.

Size *Height:* male 25–27in (63.5–68.5cm); female 24–26in (61–66cm). *Weight:* male 80lb (36kg); female 70lb (32kg).

Characteristics and Temperament
Powerful and agile, the Rhodesian Ridgeback is loyal and protective toward its family. It is not necessarily an ideal choice for the inexperienced, however.

SALUKI

The Saluki is perhaps the oldest of the domesticated dogs, and its history as a pure-bred type can be traced back thousands of years. The earliest known images of them were on carved seals from the Tepe Gawra region in what is now Kurdistan. A recent study, published in May 2004, confirms the Saluki's antiquity through DNA analysis, identifying it as one of the earliest breeds to diverge from wolves. Despite its ancient lineage, it was not seen in Europe until the 1840s.

Appearance The overall impression is one of grace and speed. The long, narrow head tapers toward the nose, which is black or liver. The muzzle is long and strong. The large eyes are a dark- to light-brown in color, conveying an intelligent, interested expression. The long, mobile ears are

The Saluki is also known as the Gazelle Hound, Arabian Hound, or Persian Greyhound, and may possibly be related to another ancient breed: the Afghan Hound.

covered in long, silky hair. The body, like the neck, is long, and the chest is deep with slightly arched ribs. Long, powerful legs and feet and a long, well-feathered tail round off the elegant appearance.

Coat Soft and silky, longer on the ears, with feathering on legs, backs of thighs and tail. Colors are white, cream, fawn, red, grizzle, silver grizzle, tricolor (black, white and tan), black-and-tan and various permutations of these colors.

Size *Height:* male 23–28in (58.5–71cm); female proportionately smaller. *Weight:* 50–66lb (23–30kg).

Characteristics and Temperament
A speedy and active hunter, with a far-sighted gaze. The breed is dignified and gentle but can become bored and destructive if left alone. Although somewhat reserved with strangers, and even highly-strung, the dog is most affectionate toward its owner.

WHIPPET

Despite appearances to the contrary, the Whippet is not a small Greyhound, but came about in the 19th century when it was made legal for working people in Britain to hunt small game and vermin. Originally called a 'snap-dog,' the term may have been coined either because of the animal's ability to snap up small game, such as rabbits, or because of the English word 'snap,' meaning food – a reference to the dog's ability to provide food for its owner. The Whippet's speed also made it a popular subject for racing,

The Whippet is a lean, muscular, athletic dog with an aerodynamically designed body. Sometimes referred to as the 'poor man's racehorse,' they are outstanding runners and are used in lure coursing, straight racing and oval-track racing. Typically, in these events, a temporary track and lure system is set up, the lure being usually a white plastic trash bag, used sometimes in conjunction with an animal pelt for its scent or a 'squawker' to simulate the sound of a prey.

and races often took place in the alleyways between houses when no other convenient venues were available.

Appearance Muscular and powerful but at the same time graceful and elegant, the head is long and lean with a tapering muzzle. The nose should be black or of a hue toning with the body-color. The oval eyes are bright and lively, and the ears are fine and rose-shaped. A long, well-muscled neck is supported by a fairly long body with a deep chest and arched loins, which give an impression of power and muscularity. The legs are long and strong. The tail is long and tapering.

Coat The coat is fine, dense and short and comes in a variety of colors and markings.

Size *Height:* male 18.5–20in (47–51cm); female 17–18.5in (43–47cm). *Weight:* 27.5–30lb (12.5–13.5kg).

Characteristics and Temperament
Specifically a sighthound, this highly adaptable sporting dog is as happy out in the field as it is at home with the family, or trotting at heel. A deservedly popular animal, it is both gentle and affectionate. The Whippet is also neat and tidy, easy to care for, and has an undemanding appetite. Although intelligent and quick to learn, perfect obedience can never be had from this breed due to its independent nature.

43

CHAPTER TWO

GUNDOGS

Dogs in this group were all bred to assist in the hunting and retrieving of game. As early as the 6th century BC, there were records of certain types of dog which, instead of pursuing game, sniffed the scent with raised head and then stood completely still. Although originally considered a rather unsatisfactory characteristic in a hunting dog, it was later realized that in fact the behavior could be very useful in the right circumstances. This was particularly the case when hunters wished to net partridge or quail, for example. Then, the dogs were trained to crouch, sit or lie down once they had spotted the game so that the hunters could draw a net over the birds before they were able to fly away.

This is the origin of the name 'bird dog,' although most gundogs today are utilized to help hunt furred quarry as well as the feathered variety. After the invention of the gun, and perhaps in recognition of the wider role the dogs played, the name of bird dog was changed to the more appropriate gundog. A gundog works in several ways: first, it must search around to locate the quarry by scent. Then it indicates its location by standing in full view and pointing – in other words, taking up a static stance and looking in the direction of the game. Next, the gundog must move forward to put the game up, which means causing the bird or other quarry to move from cover so that the hunter can shoot it. Lastly, the gundog must retrieve the game without damaging it further.

Among the features common to many gundogs are weatherproof coats that enable them to work often in wet conditions, including very cold water. In order to respond consistently and obediently to commands, gundogs must invariably be loyal, willing to please, and friendly by nature – features that makes this group the most popular of all in terms of being human companions and family pets. The stealthy nature of their work also means that they are less given to vocalization than

OPPOSITE BELOW: The English Setter was bred originally to set or point upland gamebirds, having been trained to do this in England more than 400 years ago.

RIGHT: The German Wirehaired Pointer was developed in the 1800s, becoming a leading gundog in Germany in the later part of the 20th century.

BELOW: The Red and White Irish Setter is a close relative of the Irish Setter.

hounds; again, a considerable advantage in a house dog.

Field trials are held regularly in which the qualities of the various types of gundog are tested, and certain characteristics necessary for field work, such as speed or stamina, are bred on. Sometimes these same features are considered less important in the show dog – where appearance may be more highly prized – and this explains the divergence that often occurs between the working dog and the show dog of the same breed.

Among the gundogs, different breeds are used for the various tasks in the field. The gundogs that exemplify pointing behavior include the various types of Pointer (such as the English Setter). Dogs such as the Springer Spaniel are prized for their ability to flush game from cover; some will also be expected to retrieve as well. Among the best-known of the retrieving breeds are the Golden Retriever and the Flat-Coated Retriever.

Some dogs are bred to help in all aspects of hunting. This is particularly the case in mainland Europe, where such breeds are referred to as Hunt, Point and Retrieve (HPR) breeds. These dogs include the Weimaraner from Germany, the Large Münsterlander (also from Germany) and the Italian Spinone.

BRITTANY

Originating in France, the Brittany is another Hunt, Point and Retrieve breed. Although it is often referred to as a spaniel (and, indeed, it was once called the Brittany Spaniel), the breed's working characteristics are more akin to a pointer or setter. The word 'spaniel' was dropped in the USA some years ago, when the American Brittany Club persuaded the American Kennel Club to discontinue its use. These friendly dogs have gained popularity in America and will likely soon increase their fan club in Britain, too.

Appearance Compact and square-looking, with a medium-length skull and well-

Many breeders differentiate between French and American types, although they are generally recognized as sub-sets of the same breed, even though there are differences between the two. The American Brittany is taller and faster, having been bred to cover more ground in order to hunt the wide open spaces of the United States.

defined stop. The muzzle is tapered. The expressive eyes are brown, harmonizing with the coat-color. The drop ears are set high and are rather short. The medium-length neck is carried on a deep-chested body with a short, slightly sloping back.

The legs are fairly well-boned, long and muscular, and the feet are small. These dogs are often born tailless, but when tails are present they are short or docked.

Coat Flat and dense; fine and wavy. The Brittany (Épagneul Breton) is permitted in five colors: orange-and white, liver-and-white, black-and-white, liver tricolor, and black tricolor, either in a clear or roan pattern with some ticking. The American and Canadian Kennel Clubs (AKC and CKC) do not recognize black, but all other colors are accepted worldwide and follow the FCI standard for the breed.

Size *Height:* male 19–20in (48–51cm); female 18–19in (46–48cm). *Weight:* 30–40lb (13.5–18kg).

Characteristics and Temperament
This active and energetic dog is eager to please and therefore easy to train. A good worker in the field, being able to hunt, point and retrieve, the Brittany is both intelligent and affectionate. It is very sensitive to reprimand, however; take care not to chastise it so severely that it becomes fearful and shy.

ENGLISH SETTER

One of the oldest gundog breeds – also one of the most stylish and admired, the English Setter shows evidence of a mixed ancestry involving pointers and spaniels. Development of the breed into the animal recognized today began in the mid-19th century, and was largely from stock kept pure for over 35 years. Animals from this line were crossed with others to produce dogs with temperaments better suited to hunting. English Setters were among the first pure-breds to be accepted by the American Kennel Club in 1878, the first registered being a dog named Adonis.

The elegant English Setter is the oldest of the gundogs and seems to have an innate sense of what is expected of it in the field. They are very sensitive to criticism, however, and may at times hold back for fear of disappointing their trainer. Therefore, positive reinforcement methods seem to work best for these dogs.

lemon-and-white (lemon belton), liver-and-white (liver belton), or tricolor (known as blue belton-and-tan, or liver belton-and-tan).

Size *Height:* male 25.5–27in (65–68.5cm); female 24–25.5in (61–65cm). *Weight:* male 60–66lb (27–30kg); female 56–62lb (25–28kg).

Characteristics and Temperament

A dog that excels at its task in the field, quartering the ground at speed and then setting rapidly when the quarry is located. This breed also makes a first-rate companion and pet, but may need firm training. As with most long-coated breeds, it takes time to get the dog fit for the house after a day spent out in the fields.

Appearance A dog with clean, elegant lines and with a fluid movement. The head is long with a moderately broad skull and a moderately deep and square muzzle. The nose is black or liver, depending on the coat-color, and the bright, expressive eyes are hazel to dark brown. The ears are moderately long and hang in folds. A rather long, muscular neck is carried on a body of moderate length with well-rounded ribcage. The legs are strong, muscular and well-boned. The tail is medium-length and is carried jauntily.

Coat Wavy, long and silky; shorter on the head, and with a well-feathered tail, britches and fore legs. Colors are black-and-white (known as blue belton), orange-and-white (orange belton),

Since this dog was developed to be suited to family life as well as hunting, the correct temperament is that of an intelligent, bold, and characteristically affectionate dog. Shyness, fearfulness, over-submissiveness, aloofness, lack of biddability, or aggression (especially toward human beings) are all therefore incorrect traits.

Size *Height:* male 23–25in (58.5–63.5cm); female 21–23in (53–58.5cm). *Weight:* male 55–70lb (25–32kg); female 45–60lb (20–27kg).

Characteristics and Temperament
An aristocratic-looking dog conveying an impression of alertness and energy. These are dual-purpose pointer/retrievers with a keen nose and great perseverance in the field. Rippling with muscular power, this is a dog that needs plenty of regular exercise.

GERMAN SHORTHAIRED POINTER

The origins of the breed probably stem from the stock owned by Prince Albert zu Somsbrauenfels – which were worthy but rather slow German gundogs. These were crossed with English Pointer stock, that combined the excellent scenting ability of the German dogs with the more spirited English qualities to produce a highly versatile hunt, point and retrieve gundog.

Appearance A well-balanced animal displaying power, endurance and symmetry. The head is lean and clean-cut with a broad skull and a long, strong muzzle. Depending on coat-color, the nose is solid brown or black. The brown eyes are medium-sized, with a soft and intelligent expression. The moderately long ears hang down flat. A fairly long neck is carried on a deep-chested body with a firm, short back and slightly arched loins. The legs are strong and well-boned. The tail was usually docked to a medium length, now sometimes prohibited.

Coat Short, dense and flat. Colors are solid black or solid liver; alternatively, both coat-colors may be spotted or ticked with white.

GERMAN WIREHAIRED POINTER

Created by selectively breeding certain German gundog breeds with the German Shorthair, this attractive and hardy character is a little bigger than its shorthaired cousin. This is another Hunt, Point and Retrieve breed.

Appearance The head is moderately long with a broad skull. The nose is liver or black. The medium-sized oval eyes are hazel or a darker shade. The medium-sized, rounded ears hang down. A strong neck is carried on a deep-chested body with a firm back that falls slightly toward the rear. The legs are strong and muscular. The tail is customarily docked to medium length, and is held horizontally when on the move.

Coat The functional wiry coat is the breed's most distinctive feature, and it must have a correct coat to be of the correct type. The coat is weather-resistant and, to some extent, water-repellent. The undercoat is dense enough in winter to insulate against the cold but sparse in summer as to be almost invisible. The distinctive outer coat is straight, harsh, wiry and flat-lying, and is from one to two inches in length. The outer coat is long enough to protect against the punishment of rough cover, but not so long as to hide the dog's outline. Bushy eyebrows and a full beard are desirable features. Colors are liver-and-white, solid liver, black-and-white. Solid black and tricolors are highly undesirable.

The dog is the most faithful of animals and would be much esteemed were it not so common. Our Lord God has made his greatest gift the commonest.

Martin Luther

Size *Height:* male 24–26in (61–66cm); female 22–24in (56–61cm). *Weight:* 45–75lb (20–34kg)

Characteristics and Temperament A strong, hunting breed equally capable of working in water as over ground. Being essentially a working breed, the dog requires plenty of regular exercise.

The German Wirehaired Pointer is a robust hunting dog, happy to work in water and over almost any terrain. It has a tendency to pick quarrels with other dogs, but is generally good with people and reliable where children are concerned.

GORDON SETTER

As the name implies, the Gordon Setter is of Scottish origin, bred to perfection by the Duke of Gordon in the late 18th century. Because the breed is somewhat less fashionable than the Irish or English Setters, the Gordon Setter has remained a no-nonsense, steady, working gundog, capable of working all day, if necessary.

Appearance A well-built, stylish-looking dog with a glossy coat. The head is longer than it is broad, with a moderately broad skull and a long, almost square-ended muzzle. The nose is black. The eyes are dark brown and intelligent-looking. The ears are medium-length and pendulous. The neck is long and carried on a short, deep body with slightly arched loins. Strong, moderately long, well-boned legs terminate in oval feet. The tail is long and tapers to the tip.

Coat The coat is soft and glossy, straight or slightly wavy. The hair on the ears, beneath the stomach and chest, back of legs and under the tail is long. Color is coal black with rich chestnut or tan markings.

Because the Gordon Setter has never been as fashionable as the Irish Setter it has remained far more true to type.

Size *Height:* male 26in (66cm); female 24.5in (62cm). *Weight:* male 65lb (29kg); female 56lb (25kg).

Characteristics and Temperament
The Gordon Setter is heavier and not as fast-moving as the English or Irish Setters. A bold and outgoing dog, it is a capable, trustworthy and intelligent dog, with an equable disposition. The coat needs regular grooming to maintain its condition.

HUNGARIAN VIZSLA

A native of the plains of central Hungary, the Vizsla is also sometimes called the Hungarian Pointer. The breed suffered as a result of wars in 20th-century Europe, but it was rescued from the point of extinction to become a first-class gundog – particularly useful in water – and to enjoy

considerable show success in Britain and the United States.

Appearance Medium-sized and of a distinctive and powerful appearance, the head is lean and muscular, with a moderately long skull and muzzle. The nose is brown. The slightly oval eyes should tone with the coat-color. The ears are fairly large, being a rounded V-shape and pendulous. The neck is moderately long and muscular. The back is short and well-muscled, and the chest is moderately deep. The legs are fairly long and well-boned. The tail is fairly thick, being customarily docked to two-thirds its length.

Coat Short, smooth, dense and glossy. Color is a rusty gold.

Size *Height:* male 22.5–25in (57–63.5cm); female 21–23.5in (53–60cm). *Weight:* 48.5–66lb (22–30kg).

Characteristics and Temperament
A lively and intelligent dog with great stamina, the Hungarian Vizsla is an excellent general-purpose gundog combining a good nose with stable pointing and reliable retrieving skills. The breed also makes a gentle, affectionate and protective pet, quickly adapting to all types of homes.

The Hungarian Vizsla is one of only seven recognized Hunt, Point and Retrieve (HPR) breeds. They were originally used for hunting and in falconry, but today are used as gundogs and as domestic companions.

IRISH RED AND WHITE SETTER

A close relative of the Irish Setter and arising from similar stock, one of the most famous owners of these dogs was Lord Rossmore of Monaghan, and for this reason the breed is sometimes known as the Rossmore Setter. This dog is similar in build to the Irish Setter but is altogether heavier and with a broader and more powerful head. Now gaining in popularity, the Irish Red and White Setter is undoubtedly a striking dog.

Appearance An athletic and powerful-looking dog. The head is broad in proportion with the body, with a well-defined stop. The skull is domed and the muzzle is square. The round eyes are hazel to dark brown. The ears are set well back and lie close to the head. The muscular neck is carried on a strong, muscular body with a deep chest. The legs are strong and well-muscled. The well-feathered tail is carried level with the back, or slightly below, when on the move.

Coat A fine texture coupled with good feathering are features of this coat. The coat should not be curly, although slight waviness is permitted. The base color should be white, with solid red patches, but some mottling on face, feet and lower parts of the legs is permitted.

This dog has undergone a revival in recent decades and is considered a separate breed of setter by most major kennel clubs. As of June 2007, it became eligible for AKC Miscellaneous Class conformation competition, this being a step toward full competition within the AKC.

Size *Height:* male 27in (68.5cm); female 23in (58.5cm). *Weight:* male 70lb (32kg); female 60lb (27kg).

Characteristics and Temperament
A friendly, obedient dog that proves itself equally well out in the field as in the home. It thrives best in active families and requires space to romp and exercise.

IRISH SETTER

Its striking chestnut coat makes this one of the most glamorous of the dog breeds. The dashing Irish Setter, often called the Red Setter, increased in popularity from the late 1800s onward, but little is known concerning the true origins of the breed.

Appearance A sleek and handsome dog with a racy appearance. The head is long and lean with a fairly narrow, oval skull and a long, almost square muzzle. The nose is dark brown to black. The kindly-looking eyes are dark brown. The ears are of medium length and hang in neat folds close to the head. The muscular neck is carried on a deep-chested, rather narrow body. The

The term Irish Setter is commonly used to encompass the show-bred dog recognized by the AKC as well as the field-bred Red Setter recognized by the Field Dog Stud Book. This was opened in 1874 and is the oldest registry of pure-breds in the United States.

legs are fairly long and strongly boned. The tail should be fairly long and in proportion

with the body size; it is carried level with the back, or just below, when on the move.

Coat Of moderate length, the straight, fine, glossy coat is longer on the ears, chest, tail and backs of legs. Color is mahogany or rich chestnut red with no black. A small amount of white is permitted on chest, throat or toes.

Size *Height:* male 27in (68.5cm); female 23in (58.5cm). *Weight:* male 70lb (32kg); female 60lb (27kg).

Characteristics and Temperament
Contrary to its refined appearance, the Irish Setter is an active, willing and able sporting dog, with a carefree personality. The gait while trotting is lively, graceful and

efficient. At an extended trot the head reaches slightly forward, keeping the dog in balance. More training is normally required than for other setters to ensure obedience. The breed is also hugely popular as a pet, thanks to its affectionate and playful nature. The coat needs plenty of attention to maintain its sleek and gleaming appearance.

ITALIAN SPINONE

One of the many European Hunt, Point and Retrieve breeds, the Italian Spinone has a long-established ancestry, comprising native Italian hounds crossed with French Griffons among others. The Spinone is used especially for hunting in woodland and marshy terrain. The Piedmont area of north-western Italy is primarily responsible for the development of this breed into an all-purpose dog, and it is said to outrank all other Italian gundogs as a highly efficient worker. The Spinone only achieved championship status in Britain in 1994, but in a relatively short time has earned well-deserved popularity.

Appearance A solid-looking dog with a benign expression. The head is long with a flattish skull and a squarish muzzle. The large eyes are yellow, orange or ocher, depending on coat-color. The triangular ears are pendulous and covered with short, thick hair. The neck is strong and short. The body is short and deep with a broad chest. The legs are long and well-boned. The tail is thick but usually docked to half its length.

Coat Thick and close-lying; slightly hard and wiry, with pronounced eyebrows, mustache and beard. Colors are white, or white with orange or chestnut patches or spots.

Size *Height:* male 23.5–27.5in (60–70cm); female 23–25.5in (58.5–65cm). *Weight:* male 70–82lb (32–37kg); female 62–71lb (28–32kg).

Characteristics and Temperament
An easy to train, strong, all-purpose gundog with a willing and capable disposition. The Spinone also makes a trustworthy and affectionate family pet.

Spinoni are an old breed, and some say they are descended from the Segugio Italiano, an ancient hound from the Middle Ages, while others claim they are relatives of the Barbet, Griffon and other types of Alpine hounds.

KOOIKERHONDJE

A small breed from the Netherlands, the Kooikerhondje or Kooiker Hound is a small spaniel-type that was originally a working dog, used particularly in duck hunting and tolling. There are still a few of these working decoy dogs found in Holland today, but they are mostly used for the tagging of ducks for research purposes. The dog is fairly new to the international show scene.

Appearance An attractive, medium-sized dog with a flowing coat. The moderate-sized skull and muzzle are approximately equal in length and the nose is black. The eyes are dark brown and with an alert expression. The medium-sized ears are pendulous with long feathering. A short, muscular neck is carried on a strong body with a level back and a deep chest. The legs are strong and partly feathered and terminate in hare-like feet. The tail is well-

feathered and it is carried level with the back, or slightly higher, when on the move.

Coat Of medium length and slightly wavy or straight; close-lying, with a well-developed undercoat; the topcoat has red-orange patches on a white background; a white blaze on the face is desirable. For conformation showing, dogs with black ear-tips and white tails are preferred. Tricoloration sometimes occurs, but is not a recognized variation.

Size *Height:* 14–16in (35.5–40.5cm).
Weight: 20–24lb (9–11kg).

Characteristics and Temperament
A good swimmer, the dog also has a happy, friendly and energetic nature.

Kooikers were popular in the 17th and 18th centuries and appeared in the work of Dutch painters Rembrandt and Jan Steen. The breed is rapidly gaining popularity in the United States and Canada, where it is still relatively unknown.

LARGE MÜNSTERLANDER

The Large Münsterlander had its beginnings in Münster, in Germany, where it was developed after the First World War from the same stock that was used to create the similar-looking Small Münsterlander.

Appearance A distinguished and muscular dog with an alert expression. The head is lean, the skull is moderately broad, and the muzzle is long. The nose is black. The eyes are dark brown with an intelligent expression. The ears hang flat, the hair on them extending beyond the tips. The neck is strong and muscular, sitting on a body with a strong back and a wide chest. The back is slightly higher at the shoulders and the legs

are well-muscled. The tail tapers toward the tip and is now rarely docked.

Coat Long and thick but shorter on the head; well-feathered on fore legs, hind legs and tail. The head is solid black in color, but a white blaze or star is permitted; the body is white with large black patches, flecks or ticking.

Size *Height:* male 23.5–25.5in (60–65cm); female 23–25in (58.5–63.5cm). *Weight:* 55–65lb (25–29kg).

Characteristics and Temperament
Easily trained, the dog is a good worker with an energetic, easy movement, being adaptable in all kinds of terrain, including water. The breed also makes an ideal family

companion, being loyal, affectionate and trustworthy around children.

On average, Large Münsterlanders work closer and more responsively with handlers than other gundog breeds, even though their pointing instinct matures later. They also concentrate themselves well to the task of tracking and recovering gamebirds.

NOVA SCOTIA DUCK-TOLLING RETRIEVER

The Nova Scotia Duck-Tolling Retriever comes from Canada, the first examples of the breed arriving in Britain in 1988. It was developed in the early 19th century to toll (decoy), lure and retrieve waterfowl, which it did by playing with a stick or a ball along the shoreline, thus arousing the curiosity of the ducks offshore. They were thus lured within gunshot range, following which the Toller would be sent out to retrieve the dead or wounded birds.

Appearance Richly-colored and with a compact and powerful appearance. The skull is wedge-shaped, broad, and slightly rounded, the muzzle tapering from stop to nose, which may be black or flesh-colored. The medium-sized eyes are brown or amber. The triangular-shaped ears are held slightly erect at their base. The neck is of

moderate length and well-muscled. The deep-chested body has a short back and strong, muscular loins. The legs are strong and muscular and terminate in round, strongly webbed feet – an adaptation for

swimming. The tail is well-feathered, curled over the dog's back when alert.

Coat A medium-length, double coat with a softer undercoat. The hair is straight and water-repellent. There is feathering on the throat, behind the ears, at the back of the thighs and on the fore legs. Color may be any shade of orange or red, with lighter tail feathering; white tips to the tail, feet and chest are permitted.

Size *Height:* male 19–20in (48–51cm); female 18–19in (46–48cm). *Weight:* 37.5–51lb (17–23kg).

Characteristics and Temperament
A powerful swimmer and tracker, the Duck-Toller, as it is often known, is highly intelligent, alert and ready for action, though not to the point of nervousness or hyperactivity. It also makes a good pet.

Many Tollers have slightly sad expressions until they start work, when their aspect suddenly changes to one of intense concentration and expectation.

POINTER

The Pointer is thought to have originated in Spain, but it was used in Britain from the mid-17th century to indicate, by pointing, where game was lying up. In the early 18th century, when guns came into more general use, the Pointer was further bred to improve its ability as a gundog. Excellent scenting ability, a speedy action over the ground, and a steadiness when pointing – these are all traits of the modern-day Pointer.

Appearance The breed should give the impression of compact power, agility and alertness. The head is aristocratic-looking with a moderately broad skull and a long muzzle with a concave nose-bridge. The eyes, which should have a kindly expression, are brown or hazel according to the coat-color. The ears are medium-length and pendulous. The neck is long, rounded and strong. The body is short and fairly broad with a deep chest that is carried on moderately long, strongly-boned legs. The tail is medium-length, swinging from side to side when the dog is on the move.

Coat Short, fine and hard with a glossy sheen. Colors are lemon-and-white, orange-and-white, liver-and-white and black-and-white; solid colors and tricolors are permitted.

The versatile, athletic Pointer is an excellent all-rounder, capable of all the duties required of a gundog in the field. Its every movement shows it to be an alert, hard-driving hunting dog, with the stamina, courage and desire to get to its task.

Size *Height:* male 25–27in (63.5–68.5cm); female 24–26in (61–66cm). *Weight:* male 65lb (29.5kg); female 57.5lb (26kg).

Characteristics and Temperament
This is an enthusiastic and able worker with enormous powers of speed and endurance. The Pointer also fits in well with family life, being well-mannered, intelligent and affectionate.

CHESAPEAKE BAY RETRIEVER

During the early part of the 19th century two puppies, reported as Newfoundlands in type, were rescued from a shipwreck off the coast of Maryland, USA. These dogs were mated with local retrievers, the crossings being the beginning of the breed known as the Chesapeake Bay Retriever. The dog was used to retrieve ducks in the cold waters of Chesapeake Bay, and it was suitably adapted for this purpose by virtue of its thick, oily, waterproof coat. A layer of subcutaneous fat also helped keep out the cold, adding to the breed's impression of solidity.

Appearance A strong, muscular dog with a distinctive coat. The skull is broad with a shortish, relatively broad muzzle. The nose color should harmonize with the coat, the eyes being yellow or amber. The small ears hang loosely at the sides of the head. The muscular neck tapers from the head to the shoulders. The body is of medium length with a deep chest. The strong, medium-length legs terminate in webbed hare-like feet. The tail is heavy and strong and can be straight or slightly curved.

Coat Short and thick with a dense, woolly undercoat. The coat is oily and able to repel water. The coat may be any color, ranging from dark brown to faded tan to the color of dead grass.

Size *Height:* male 23–26in (58.5–66cm); female 21–24in (53–61cm). *Weight:* male 65–80lb (29–36kg); female 55–70lb (25–32kg).

Characteristics and Temperament
Essentially a duck dog, and in its element when working in water, the Chesapeake Bay Retriever is willing, courageous and independent. It also makes a good guardian and companion – albeit one with a very hearty appetite.

Chesapeakes are naturally dominant dogs and although they might not actually start a fight, they will defend their position as the alpha dog. Obedience training is therefore a must with this breed.

CURLY-COATED RETRIEVER

The breed arose as the result of crossings between water spaniels, various types of retrievers and, possibly, pointers. The tight, curly coat was probably enhanced by adding poodle stock to the breeding program. The breed reached the peak of its popularity in the latter half of the 19th century, when many were taken to Australia and New Zealand to be used for hunting birds. The unique coat is well-adapted for work in the water and soon dries out.

Appearance A strong, elegant-looking dog with a dark, curly coat. The head is long and wedge-shaped with a fairly broad skull and longish muzzle. The nose is black in dogs with black fur and brown in brown-furred dogs. The eyes are large and, again, should harmonize with the coat-color. The pendulous ears are rather small and lie close to the head. The strong neck is carried on a broad body with a deep chest. The legs are strong and muscular, terminating in round feet. The tail is long.

Coat The coat is a mass of small, tight curls extending over most of the body apart from the face and skull. Coat-colors are black or liver.

Size *Height:* male 27in (68.5cm); female 25in (63.5cm). *Weight:* 70–80lb (32–36kg).

Characteristics and Temperament
In the field, the Curly-Coated Retriever is

Developed in England, the Curly was long a favorite of English gamekeepers. This multi-purpose hunting retriever is recognized by most canine historians as one of the oldest of the retrieving breeds.

adept at marking where fallen game is lying and retrieving it. An intelligent dog with great stamina and confidence, the breed is happiest when leading an active life in the open – preferably around water. Nevertheless, it is a friendly and loyal dog.

FLAT-COATED RETRIEVER

A blend of the St. John's Newfoundland (a smaller version of the Newfoundland) and spaniels, setters and sheepdogs, the breed was first shown in Britain in 1859. Less popular than other types of gundog for some years, there is now growing interest in the Flat-Coated Retriever, which has the lightest build of all the retrievers.

Appearance A medium-sized dog with an intelligent expression and an active nature. The head is long, with a medium-to-broad skull and a longish muzzle. The eyes are dark brown to hazel. The ears are small

and close-fitting to the sides of the head. The body has a rather broad, deep chest, and moderately long, strongly-boned legs terminate in rounded feet with thick paw-pads. The tail is fairly short and is carried jauntily, but seldom above the level of the back.

Coat The coat is dense, of fine to medium texture and as flat as possible. Colors are black or liver.

Size *Height:* male 23–24in (58.5–61cm); female 22–23in (56–58.5cm). *Weight:* male 60–80lb (27–36kg); female 55–70lb (25–32kg).

Characteristics and Temperament
The Flat-Coated Retriever matures slowly, retaining its puppy-like quality for years on end. This is a cheerful and playful extrovert that enjoys the companionship of human beings yet is a good guard dog when required. In the field, the dog works effectively and it is a capable and enthusiastic swimmer.

The most important and distinctive features of the Flat-Coated Retriever is the silhouette (both when moving and standing), the smooth effortless motion, and the long, strong, clean, head, that is one of a piece and unique to the breed.

GOLDEN RETRIEVER

The Golden Retriever is thought to have originated from a first crossing between a yellow wavy-coated retriever and a spaniel, with subsequent matings with setters and other retrievers. These dogs were first known as Retrievers (Golden or Yellow), but in 1920 received their present name of Golden Retriever. One of the most versatile of breeds, and also one of the most popular, it is used to retrieve game in the field, for detecting drugs and explosives, as a tracker and guide dog – and last but not least, as a favorite family dog. According to the American Kennel Club, the Golden Retriever, with its sharp intelligence and eager-to-please attitude, is

and cat-like. The muscular tail is carried level with the back; it is used by the animal for steering itself when swimming.

Coat The coat is flat or wavy and well-feathered; the undercoat is dense and water-resistant. Color may be any shade of cream or gold.

Size *Height:* male 22–24in (56–61cm); female 20–22in (51–56cm). *Weight:* male 70–80lb (32–36kg); female 60–70lb (27–32kg).

Characteristics and Temperament
This is not only an intelligent dog with great natural ability, but it is also relatively easy to train. The Golden Retriever possesses a confident, friendly and patient temperament and makes an enthusiastic pet – wagging its tail energetically to express its pleasure.

Every boy should have two things: a dog, and a mother willing to let him have one.

Anonymous

today one of the most popular breeds in the USA.

Appearance The head has a broad skull with a powerful, wide, deep muzzle. The nose is black, and the eyes are dark brown with a kindly expression. The ears are moderately large and hang flat. A clean, muscular neck is carried on a shortish body with deep ribs. The legs are moderately long and well-boned, and the feet are round

The Golden Retriever originated in the Scottish Highlands in the late 1800s and was used predominantly for hunting. It was developed with the intention of creating a superb retriever suited to the Scottish climate, terrain and available game.

LABRADOR RETRIEVER

The Labrador Retriever is believed to have its origins in Greenland, where similar dogs were once used by fishermen to retrieve fish. It was introduced into Britain in the late 1800s, where it made its reputation in field trials. The breed club for these dogs was started comparatively recently, in 1916, with the Yellow Labrador club being formed in 1925. One the best-known and popular breeds in the world today, the dog is a great all-rounder, being employed for a variety of working roles, also as a companion.

Appearance Instantly recognizable, the overall impression is of a strongly-built, active dog. The head has a broad skull with a broad, medium-length muzzle. The eyes are brown or hazel, and express intelligence and good nature. The ears are set fairly far back on the head and hang flat. The strong neck is carried on a body with a broad, deep chest. The legs are well-developed. The tail is thick and broad and covered in short, dense fur, giving it a rounded appearance.

Coat The distinctive coat is short and dense and feels fairly hard to the touch; the undercoat is waterproof. Colors may be solid black, yellow or chocolate (liver).

Size *Height:* male 22–22.5in (56–57cm); female 21.5–22in (54.5–56cm). *Weight:* male 60–75lb (27–34kg); female 55–70lb (25–32kg).

Characteristics and Temperament
An intelligent, soft-mouthed retriever with a willingness to work and a love of water. Happiest in the countryside, it nevertheless makes an adaptable, devoted family pet.

Possibly the most popular breed in the world, the Labrador is by far the favorite in the US (since 1991), the UK, Poland, and several other countries. It is also the most popular breed of assistance dog in the US, Australia and elsewhere, and is widely used by police and other official bodies for its detection and working abilities.

AMERICAN COCKER SPANIEL

This attractive dog was bred in America in the 19th century from Cocker Spaniels imported from Britain, its main job being to retrieve gamebirds such as quail. The smallest of the gundog group, the American Cocker is a sound and willing worker, but today, this long-coated breed is more often seen in the show ring or family home than working in the field. Exhibited in the US since the 1880s, the Cocker remains one of the most popular breeds in North America.

Appearance A distinctive, smallish, neat dog with a full coat on the legs and abdomen. The head is shortish and refined, with a rounded skull and a deep, broad muzzle. The nose should be black in black-and-tans and brown or black in dogs of other colors. The eyes are full and round with a forward-looking gaze; the expression should be alert and appealing. The ears are long and lobe-shaped and are covered in long fur. The neck is long and muscular. The body is short and compact with a deep chest; the back slopes slightly from withers to tail. The legs are strong and muscular. The tail is usually docked by three-fifths of its length.

Coat The medium-length coat is silky and flat or slightly wavy; shorter on the head. The dog comes in various colors including solid black and black-and-tan.

Size *Height:* male 14.5–15.5in (37–39.5cm); female 13.5–14.5in (34–37cm). *Weight:* 24–28.5lb (11–13kg).

Characteristics and Temperament
A keen and happy dog with a friendly and confident manner, the breed makes an excellent family pet. The profuse coat needs regular grooming to keep it looking its best.

Derived from the same stock as its English cousin, the American Cocker Spaniel has evolved so differently that it is now recognized as a separate breed.

ENGLISH COCKER SPANIEL

One of the oldest spaniel breeds, the dog's original name of Cocking Spaniel derived from its use for flushing woodcocks from cover. Soon after the Kennel Club of Great Britain was formed in 1873, Cocker Spaniels were recognized as a separate breed from Springer Spaniels and Field Spaniels. Cockers used for work are less sturdy and less heavy than their counterparts seen in the show ring. This is the most popular of the spaniel breeds.

Appearance The overall impression is of a merry, compact, well-balanced sporting dog. The skull must not be too broad or long, and the muzzle must be square with a distinct stop. The eyes are dark brown or a lighter brown or hazel, toning with the coat; the expression is intelligent, alert but gentle. The ears are lobe-shaped, thin and pendulous. A muscular, medium-length neck is carried on a strong, compact body with a well-developed chest. The dog has short, strongly-boned legs and cat-like feet. The tail is usually docked, but never so short that it impedes the dog's non-stop action when on the move.

Coat Flat and silky; well-feathered fore legs, hind legs (above hocks) and body. Various colors are available; self-colors should only have white on the chest.

The Cocker is full of charm, matched with good looks and a lively personality. It needs all the exercise it can get, but be careful to remove tangles after a walk in the woods.

Size *Height:* male 15.5–16in (39.5–41cm); female 15–15.5in (38–39.5cm). *Weight:* 28–32lb (13–14.5kg).

Characteristics and Temperament
A most willing and happy dog. The Cocker Spaniel is quick to adapt to its surroundings and is equally at home sniffing around in the countryside as it is playing indoors with its family. The breed enjoys exercise and company and is fond of carrying things about in its mouth.

ENGLISH SPRINGER SPANIEL

Formerly known as the Norfolk Spaniel, this pure and ancient breed was awarded official status in 1902. The breed gets the name 'springer' from the fact that this type of spaniel was used to flush birds into the air from cover so that they would spring upward and thus be bagged by the hunters.

Appearance A compact, racy dog of symmetrical build that stands high on the leg. The medium-length skull is fairly broad, and the muzzle is also rather broad and deep. The almond-shaped eyes, of hazel coloration, have a kind and alert expression. The ears are lobe-shaped, fairly long, and hang flat. The neck is long, strong and muscular. The body is strong with a deep chest and is carried on well-developed legs.

The tail, customarily docked, is well-feathered and has a lively action.

Coat Long, dense and soft but also tough and weather-resistant; feathering on ears, fore legs, belly and hindquarters. Colors are black-and-white, liver-and-white, or these colors with tan markings.

Size *Height:* 20in (51cm). *Weight:* 47lb (21kg).

Characteristics and Temperament
A friendly and extrovert gundog, willing to search for, flush, and retrieve game – even in icy water. It makes an affectionate family dog, albeit one that likes plenty of exercise.

A field-bred Springer and one that has been bred for showing are breeds apart, and could never swap roles; in fact, the gene pools have become almost completely segregated and have been for at least 70 years.

FIELD SPANIEL

The breed arose as a result of crossings between the Sussex Spaniel and the Cocker Spaniel. The Field Spaniel has enjoyed mixed fortunes; the breed almost disappeared in the early 1900s and again in the 1950s. At one time, its numbers were so small that the UK Kennel Club would not allow it championship status. However,

determined efforts by enthusiasts and breeders reversed this decision in the 1960s.

Appearance A dog built for activity and endurance and one with a noble character. The head has a broad, long skull and a lean muzzle. The almond-shaped eyes are dark hazel in color and have a gentle expression. The moderately long ears are set low and are well-feathered. The neck is long and

muscular. The body has a level and strong back and a deep chest. The medium-length legs terminate in round feet. The tail is docked by one-third and should not be carried higher than the back.

Coat Flat, glossy and silky, weatherproof and dense; a well-feathered chest, underbody and hind legs. Colors are black, liver, golden-liver, mahogany or roan; any

A rare combination of beauty and utility, the Field Spaniel is a well-balanced, substantial hunter-companion of medium size, built for activity and endurance both in heavy cover and in water.

of these colors with tan markings are permitted, as are white or roan on the chests of solid-colored dogs.

Size *Height:* 18in (46cm). *Weight:* 40–55lb (18–25kg).

Characteristics and Temperament

An active gundog, but placid, obedient and intelligent. Not recommended for the town-dweller, however, since the Field Spaniel really belongs where its name suggests – out in the open countryside.

IRISH WATER SPANIEL

This is a very ancient breed, but there is some disagreement among experts as to its true ancestry. What is undeniable, however, is that the Water Spaniel is a versatile worker in the field as well as a good companion. This is the tallest of the spaniel breeds.

Appearance A large and purposeful-looking spaniel with a distinctive curly coat. The skull is high-domed and fairly broad and long, and the muzzle is long and strong. The nose is dark liver in color. The eyes have an alert expression and are amber to dark brown. The long ears are oval-shaped and pendulous. The neck is powerful and arched and is carried on a short, deep body. The legs are long and strongly boned and terminate in large feet. The tail is fairly long and tapers to a point.

Coat Composed of dense, crisp, tight ringlets and with a natural oiliness that facilitates the dog's ability to retrieve from water; the coat is shorter on the muzzle, throat and lower part of the tail. Color is a rich, dark liver.

Size *Height:* male 21–23in (53–58.5cm); female 20–22in (51–56cm). *Weight:* male

The Irish Water Spaniel, as we know it today, was developed to hunt, flush and retrieve snipe and wildfowl from the bogs, marshes and river estuaries of Ireland, which led to its nickname of 'bogdog.'

55–65lb (25–29kg); female 45–58lb (20–26kg).

Characteristics and Temperament
A useful gundog, especially where retrieval from water is required. Although sometimes described as reserved, the breed is affectionate and faithful, and its admirers talk of the dog's great sense of humor. Thorough grooming is required.

SUSSEX SPANIEL

The breed first arose in Sussex, England, over 120 years ago. The Sussex Spaniel, like the Field Spaniel, in whose foundation the Sussex Spaniel was involved, is rarely seen today, having become less fashionable than the more lightly-built breeds of spaniel popular today.

Appearance A long-bodied, powerfully-built dog with a heavy brow. The head is medium-long with a broad skull and a long, square muzzle. The nose is liver. The large hazel eyes have a gentle expression. The ears are thick and lobular and hang flat to the head. The neck is long and strong and is carried on a deep and muscular body. The well-boned legs are rather short. The tail is usually docked and has a lively action.

Coat An abundant, flat coat with profuse feathering on the forequarters and hindquarters. The permitted coat-color is golden-liver and eyes must be hazel.

Size *Height:* 15–16in (38–41cm). *Weight:* 39.5–51lb (18–23kg).

Characteristics and Temperament
The Sussex Spaniel has a characteristic rolling gait when on the move. It is also unusual among spaniels in being quite vocal when working. Despite its heavy appearance, the breed is energetic, while at the same time being docile and friendly.

The Sussex Spaniel was among the first ten breeds to be recognized and admitted to the stud book when the American Kennel Club was formed in 1884, although it had existed as a distinct breed for much longer, having been used in England since the 18th century.

WELSH SPRINGER SPANIEL

Red-and-white spaniels closely resembling the Welsh Springer Spaniel had existed for many years before they were recognized as a breed by the UK Kennel Club in 1902. Slightly lighter in build than the English Springer, the Welsh was used extensively for hunting but nowadays is seen increasingly at shows. Imported into the US in the late 1800s, the breed was recognized by the AKC in 1906.

Appearance A compact and attractively marked dog, similar to, but slightly smaller than, the English Springer. The head is of moderate length, the skull being slightly domed and with a medium-length muzzle. The nose is flesh-colored or darker; the AKC considers a pink nose undesirable, although in Britain it is recognized, and was probably the original type. Eyes are hazel or dark brown with a kindly expression. The ears are fairly small and hang flat. The neck is long and muscular. The body is strong and muscular. Medium-length, well-boned legs terminate in round, cat-like feet. The tail is usually docked and has a lively action.

Coat Straight, thick and silky; feathering occurs on the fore legs, hind legs above the hocks, and on the ears and tail. Color is a striking red and white.

Size *Height:* male 19in (48cm); female 18in (46cm). *Weight:* 34–45lb (15–20kg).

Characteristics and Temperament
A dog built to work hard without tiring, being fast and active in its movements. The Welsh Springer Spaniel also makes an obedient and friendly house pet.

The body of the Welsh Springer tends to give a false impression of length, due to its obliquely angled forequarters and well-developed hindquarters.

WEIMARANER

The Weimaraner gets its name from the German court of Weimar, where the dog was very popular. Dogs of similar appearance, albeit more hound-like in appearance, were depicted from the early 1600s by the painter Van Dyck. The dog has proved effective in Hunt, Point and Retrieve duties, having originally been used to hunt boar and deer, although today it accompanies hunters looking for smaller game. The most commonly seen version is the shorthaired variety, but there is also a longhaired form.

Appearance A tall, elegant and purposeful-looking dog with unusual coloration. The head is fairly long and aristocratic with a long muzzle. The nose is gray. The eyes are round and vary in color from amber to blue-gray. The ears are long, taper to a point, and are slightly folded. A moderately

long neck is carried on a rather long body with a deep chest, and the legs are strong and well-boned. The tail is docked.

Coat Short and sleek. In the longhaired variety, the fur is 1–2-in (2.5–5-cm) long, with feathering on the tail and backs of the legs. Color is silver-gray, mouse- or roe-gray with a metallic sheen. According to the American Kennel Club standard, a distinctly blue or black coat is an automatic disqualification, although a small white patch on the chest area is permitted.

Size *Height:* male 24–27in (61–68.5cm); female 22–25in (56–63.5cm). *Weight:* male 59.5lb (27kg); female 49.5lb (22.5kg).

Characteristics and Temperament
An able multi-role hunting dog which is fearless but friendly and obedient. Increasingly, the breed is also finding favor as a domestic companion.

Weimaraners are suitable home animals given the appropriate training and exercise. They are not as friendly toward strangers as other hunting dogs, but are protective of their family. They are inclined to be territorial.

CHAPTER THREE
TERRIERS

The word 'terrier' comes from *terra*, the Latin word for earth, and aptly describes that aspect of the landscape in which these dogs were originally utilized – having being bred to drive badgers, foxes, rabbits and other quarry from their underground retreats. On occasions, when the terrier was unable to penetrate the burrow or earth, it was still able to indicate the presence of the quarry to the hunter, who would then unearth and dispatch it by other means.

Because of the qualities needed to perform these tasks, most terriers are small to medium-sized dogs, often with powerful jaws and short legs that are great for digging; they also have huge amounts of courage and tenacity. In time, the name terrier also came to be applied to dogs that were kept for dispatching vermin, such as rats and mice.

Because different sorts of terriers were required for working over many varied kinds of terrain, cross-breeding with other types of dog became common practice. Thus breeds of terrier required to keep up with huntsmen on horseback might be bred

RIGHT: The Airedale is the largest of the terriers, originally developed to hunt otters, badgers and wolves. It is a lively and adaptable dog that needs firm but kind handling.

OPPOSITE: The Border Terrier is a tough, active little dog, being one of the smallest of the working terriers.

with hounds to improve their stamina and increase the length of the legs, while terriers used for fighting would be bred with mastiffs and other large, powerful dogs to improve their skills in combat. Many of these new terrier breeds arose because of local needs, and often bear the name of the place where they originated. The Manchester Terrier, the Skye Terrier and the Australian Terrier, for example, leave no doubt as to their origins.

The rise in the popularity of terriers began in the latter part of the 19th century when dog shows introduced many of these animals to a wider audience; this was also the period when many of the breed standards were formulated. As with many other breeds, shows today tend to concentrate on appearance, and terriers have often been among the top award-winners around the world.

Terriers range in size from the largest, the Airedale Terrier (which is 24in /61cm at the shoulder) to the much smaller Norfolk Terrier (which stands only 10-in/25.5-cm high). Despite these great differences in size, terriers usually exhibit many shared characteristics: they are naturally alert and curious dogs, being sharp in movement, their ancestry compelling them to dig holes in the ground whenever and wherever they can – an alarming propensity of great concern to owners with well-kept gardens.

On the whole, terriers are robust dogs, and less sensitive than many other pedigree breeds. For this reason, they make good pets for a young growing family. They are usually easy for young children to pick up and cuddle, are always ready for action and to join in a game; also, they don't take it too personally when scolded for doing wrong. They can, however, be a little too ready to pick fights with any other dogs they may encounter, on occasions tending to charge straight in without warning.

About two thirds of the world's terrier breeds originated in Britain. Some breeds of terrier are not classed in the main terrier group, but in other groups such as the toy dogs or the utility group. Furthermore, the so-called Tibetan Terrier is not a terrier at all, being related to the working dogs.

Terrier breeds require their coats to be regularly clipped or trimmed – often referred to as stripping – to retain their classic, strong-lined appearance. This is usually carried out professionally twice-yearly, although for show purposes more detailed preparation is usually required.

AIREDALE

This breed, by far the largest of the terriers (and sometimes called the King of Terriers for this reason), originated in Yorkshire, England. The dog reflects both terrier and hound ancestry in its makeup and behavior, although it is too big to go underground in the traditional manner. The Airedale's imposing size means that it is occasionally used as a guard dog among other duties.

Appearance A muscular, cobby and active-looking dog. The head is long and flat and not too broad between the ears. The nose is black, and the dark eyes have a lively expression. The V-shaped ears are small, folded, and placed high at the sides of the head. The neck is muscular and is carried on a body with a short, strong and level back; the chest is deep. The legs are long and well-boned. The tail is strong and carried high; it is customarily docked.

Coat The texture is hard, wiry and dense; the undercoat is softer. The color is tan, with a black or grizzle saddle, top of neck and top of tail.

Size *Height:* male 23–24in (58.5–61cm); female 22–23in (56–58.5cm). *Weight:* 45lb (20.5kg).

Characteristics and Temperament
The Airedale's remarkable scenting powers

Airdales were used extensively in the First World War to carry dispatches to soldiers behind enemy lines, and there are numerous tales of them delivering their messages despite terrible injuries. They were also used by the Red Cross to seek out soldiers lying wounded on the battlefield.

mean that it is used for tracking, for detecting victims in collapsed buildings, and for game-hunting. It also comes into its own as an intelligent and courageous guard dog. The breed also makes a devoted and protective family pet, always ready to join in the next game or simply accompany its owner out on a walk. Despite its size it is not a huge eater, but it has a healthy apetite nonetheless.

AUSTRALIAN TERRIER

Thought to have been bred from British terriers imported into Australia by early settlers, the Australian Terrier achieved show recognition in Britain in 1936. This is one of very few terrier breeds to have originated outside Britain.

Appearance A low-set, longish dog with a rough coat and a 'ready-for-action' look about it. The head is long with a flat skull and a longish muzzle. The nose is black. The dark-brown eyes are small and have a keen expression. The small ears are pricked and free from long hair. The neck is long and slightly arched. The body is quite long

in proportion with the dog's height, and it is fairly deep-chested. The legs are quite short, and the tail is usually docked.

Coat Long, straight and hard to the touch. There are two colors: the coat may be blue, steel-blue, or dark blue-gray with tan on the face, ears, underbody, lower legs and

The Australian Terrier's talents as a rat- and snake-catcher may no longer be to the fore, but it still retains the innate pluckiness and tenacity that is the hallmark of the breed.

feet; the topknot is blue or silver. Alternatively the coat may be sandy or red, with a topknot of a lighter shade.

Size *Height:* 10in (25.5cm). *Weight:* 14lb (6.3kg).

Characteristics and Temperament

A bright, lively little dog with a hardy constitution. The breed likes exercise and play and makes a cheerful and affectionate pet, being always anxious to please.

BEDLINGTON TERRIER

A dog with one of the longest traceable pedigrees of any terrier, the Bedlington hails from Rothbury in northeast England – indeed, its original name was the Rothbury Terrier. The high-arched back suggests some Whippet blood in its ancestry, among other breeds. It was originally bred for the purpose of catching food, such as rabbits for the pot, and the breed remains a tough and spirited performer despite its lamb-like appearance.

Appearance A graceful and muscular dog with a large, wedge-shaped head. The skull is narrow, deep and rounded. The eyes are small, bright and triangular, the color varying with the coat-color. The ears are moderately long and hang down flat to the cheeks. The neck is long and tapering, carried on a long, muscular body with a deep chest and arched back and loins. The legs are moderately long and end in hare-like feet. The tail is long and tapering and is never held over the back.

Coat Thick and with a characteristic texture described as 'linty.' The non-shedding coat is usually trimmed to produce the appearance so distinctive of the breed. Colors are blue, sandy, liver, or dark brown/black and sable, and there can be solid-color coats or coats with tan markings. These become paler as the dog matures, but should never be pure white;

Despite its unusual appearance, the Bedlington is far from lamb-like, and has all the qualities desirable in a champion ratter.

this indicates a lack of guard hairs, which are what gives the coat its texture and protective properties.

Size *Height:* 16in (41cm). *Weight:* 18–23lb (8–10.5kg).

Characteristics and Temperament
Its gentle and unusual appearance belies its true terrier nature. The Bedlington moves with a unique, light movement, as if it were floating above the ground.

BORDER TERRIER

The Border Terrier originated in the border region between England and Scotland, although the name is probably a reference to the fact that the dog worked with the Border Foxhounds. The present name was adopted in the early part of the 19th century, but the breed was not recognized by the UK Kennel Club until 1920. A true worker, the dog was bred to enter foxes' lairs to flush out their occupants; the dogs also needed to be able to keep up with riders on horseback.

Appearance A tough, no-nonsense little dog with typical terrier attributes. The head is shaped like that of an otter but with a broad skull and a short, strong muzzle. The nose is black, liver or flesh-colored. The dark eyes have an alert expression. The ears are small, V-shaped and folded. The strong neck is carried on a deep, narrow and fairly long body. The legs are moderately long. The tail is fairly short and carried high but not over the back.

Coat Thick and harsh with a dense undercoat. Colors are red, wheaten, tan-and-grizzle or tan-and-blue.

Size *Height:* male 12in (30.5cm); female 11in (28cm). *Weight:* male 13–15.5lb (6–7kg); female 11–14lb (5–6.5kg).

Characteristics and Temperament
The dog is as it appears, being a strong, well-boned and active little terrier whose job it is to go to ground to flush out foxes. Its legs are sufficiently long for it to keep up with riders on horseback, yet the dog is small enough to be picked up when necessary. It has strong jaws and a chest narrow enough to allow it to move in and out of lairs. Despite these workmanlike qualities, the Border Terrier also makes a kindly and adaptable family pet. Borders will adapt to the activity levels of their owners; they do not demand exercise, but appreciate it when they get it.

The workmanlike Border Terrier has a happy-go-lucky nature and, despite it having been bred as a hunter, is still able to adapt happily to family life.

BULL TERRIER

The Bull Terrier was first bred in Birmingham, England, by crossing dogs with bulldog and terrier blood with English White Terriers. Standardization of the breed is accredited to James Hinks, and the Bull Terrier Club was formed in 1887. The breed has a unique appearance, but unfortunately has also gained a reputation for pugnacious behavior. Today, however, breeders have succeeded in producing an animal with a more sociable attitude toward other dogs. A miniature Bull Terrier also exists; this is almost identical in appearance to the standard Bull Terrier, but is only 14in (35.5cm) in height.

Appearance A muscular, stocky dog with a characteristic egg-shaped head. The long, strong head has powerful jaws and a gently sloping profile from the top of the head down to the nose-tip. The nose is black. The eyes are narrow, triangular and slanting. The ears are small and pricked. The neck is long and muscular. The dog has a very broad chest when viewed from the front and a short, strong back. The legs are moderately long with strong bones. The tail is short and carried horizontally.

Coat Short, flat and harsh but glossy. Acceptable colors for show dogs are white, (skin pigmentation and markings on the head are not penalized in the UK show ring), any color other than white, or any color with white markings (although blue and liver are highly undesirable).

The American Temperament Test Society (ATTS), a non-profit-making organization that promotes uniform temperament among dog breeds, gives the Bull Terrier a pass rate of 92.1 per cent, the average for all breeds being 81.5 per cent.

Size *Height:* 18in (46cm). *Weight:* 72lb (33kg).

Characteristics and Temperament
Despite the Bull Terrier's rather intimidating appearance (it stands four-square in a manner not unlike a bull, from which its name is partly derived) it is in fact usually well-disposed toward human beings. In fact they have been described as friendly dogs with a good sense of humor, and could even be said to behave clownishly at times. They are not ideal pets for a first-time owner, however, and often need firm handling to ensure a peaceful co-existence with other dogs; they can also be rather obstinate at times.

CAIRN TERRIER

The Highlands of Scotland and the Isle of Skye were the original home of the Cairn Terrier, where it was bred for hunting otters, badgers and foxes rather than for its appearance. Cairns are still used as working dogs in parts of Scotland, and many retain this independent spirit which precludes them from being good lap dogs. The breed was first shown in 1909, although dogs of this type can be traced back over 500 years.

Appearance A game little dog with a wiry, slightly unkempt 'varminty' look. The head is small with a broad skull and a powerful muzzle. The nose is black. The hazel eyes are deep-set and protected by shaggy eyebrows. The small, pointed ears are pricked. The compact body is strong, with a deep chest and a level back. The legs are short and strongly-boned.

Coat A thick, harsh outercoat with a short, close undercoat. The tail is short and well-covered with hair. Colors are cream, red, wheaten, gray or nearly black, all of which may be brindled, usually changing to a darker shade during the dog's lifetime. Ears and muzzle may be darker than the coat.

Size *Height:* 11–12in (28–30.5cm). *Weight:* 14–16lb (6–7.5kg).

Characteristics and Temperament
An alert and endearingly mischievous dog, the Cairn Terrier is fearless and ready for anything. Although it is often said that they are disobedient, this can be remedied provided the correct training is applied.

Through cross-breeding, the Cairn has over the years contributed elements of its vibrant personality to other terriers.

CESKY

The Cesky Terrier (Bohemian Terrier) was bred to hunt rats and foxes in their dens. They were first imported into the US in about 1987.

Appearance A short-legged dog, rather long in the body compared with its height. The head is fairly long and has a slightly arched skull. The nose is black in blue-gray dogs or liver in brown dogs. Eyes are black or brown depending on the coat-color. The ears are triangular and pendulous. The powerful, medium-length neck is arched. The body is long with a level back, and there is a slight rise over the loins. The legs are short but muscular. The tail is long and is carried slightly raised when on the move.

Coat The wavy coat has a silken sheen and is usually clipped, except on the upper part of the head, legs and underbody. Electric clippers are used instead of the more usual coat-stripping technique. Colors are blue-gray or light brown.

The Cesky exists due to the efforts of Czech breeder, František Horák, being a mixture of Sealyham and Scottish terriers.

Size *Height:* 11–14in (28–35.5cm). *Weight:* male 17.5lb (8kg); female 15.5lb (7kg).

Characteristics and Temperament
Tough, hardy and agile, the Cesky Terrier is a somewhat wary, yet nevertheless friendly dog. Like most terriers, they are feisty, stubborn and fearless, but they love children and like to guard the house.

DANDIE DINMONT

The fictional character Dandie Dinmont, from the novel *Guy Mannering* by Sir Walter Scott, is the inspiration for the name of this breed, although dogs of this type existed in the border region of England and Scotland long before the story appeared. The dog was originally developed for hunting otters and badgers.

Appearance A dog with a ferret-like body, short legs, and a large, distinctive head. The head has a large, almost square skull and a deep muzzle. The nose is black. The dark hazel eyes are large and expressive. The ears are pendulous. The strong and muscular neck is carried on a long, deep body with well-arched loins. The legs are short and heavily-boned, the hind legs being a little longer than the fore legs. The tail is short.

Coat A double coat with a soft undercoat and a hard, crisp, topcoat; fore legs are feathered; the head is covered with soft, silky fur. Colors are pepper or mustard.

Size *Height:* 8–11in (20–28cm). *Weight:* 18–24lb (8–11kg).

Characteristics and Temperament
The Dandie Dinmont has the ability to perform its working function while at the same time being a devoted and affectionate pet – albeit a rather willful one.

Today the Dandie Dinmont is one of the rarest and most endangered of all pure breeds/pedigree dogs, listed by the UK Kennel Club as a Vulnerable Native Dog Breed, there being a real chance of it becoming extinct.

SMOOTH-HAIRED FOX TERRIER

This is one of the most popular and well-established of all the terriers. It originated in Britain and has an ancestry that is probably linked with Bull Terriers and Manchester Terriers. The standard for the breed was drawn up in the 1870s. This terrier is a valuable addition to the foxhound pack, being small enough to

chase foxes from cover which is too inaccessible to be reached by larger dogs. Although fashionable in the show ring, the breed has remained true to its original type. It was long held that the Smooth Fox Terrier and Wirehaired Fox Terrier are variations of the same breed; in recent years, however, experts have increasingly being saying that the two are not related at all. Whereas the Wire Fox Terrier is

probably directly descended from the rough black-and-tan terrier used in Wales, the Smooth Fox Terrier is thought to count the Manchester Terrier as its primary ancestor, also with traces of Bull Terrier and Beagle thrown in.

Appearance A compact and purposeful-looking dog. The skull is flat and rather narrow, and the muzzle is long and strong. The nose is black. The eyes are small and dark with an alert, intelligent expression. The drop ears are V-shaped. The neck looks clean with no dewlap. The body is deep-chested, with a short, level back. The hind legs give potency to the dog's movements, and must be strong and muscular with a good length. The tail is docked and carried jauntily.

Coat Smooth, short, hard and dense. Preferred colors are all-white, black-and-white, or tan-and-white.

Size *Height:* male 15.5in (39.5cm); female proportionately smaller. *Weight:* male 16–18lb (7–8kg); female 15–17lb (7–7.5kg).

Characteristics and Temperament Large enough to cope with foxes and strong enough to run with the hunt, the Smooth is lively and eager. The breed needs a firm hand as far as discipline is concerned, but rewards a caring owner with devotion and affection. Not usually one to start an argument with another dog, the breed will nevertheless give a good account of itself once provoked.

Like most terriers, the Smooth-Haired Fox Terrier is inclined to be stubborn. Training is relatively simple but owners must be consistent and firm. These dogs like to bark and dig, and must be trained to stop these actions on command.

WIREHAIRED FOX TERRIER

It is likely that the Wirehaired Fox Terrier was developed before its Smooth counterpart, although it was the latter that appeared first in the show ring. The Wirehaired was originally called the Rough-Haired Terrier. A popular family dog, the breed appears at its best when trimmed to the classic shape.

Appearance A compact and well-balanced dog. The skull is flat, rather narrow, and slightly sloping. The muzzle is long and strong and the nose is black. The eyes are small and dark indicating alertness and

intelligence. The small drop ears are V-shaped and moderately thick. The neck is fairly long, lean and muscular. The body has a deep chest and a short, level back. The legs are strong and muscular. The tail is docked and carried erect.

Coat Wiry and dense with an undercoat of shorter, softer hair. Color is mainly white with black, tan, or black-and-tan markings.

Size *Height:* male 15.5in (39.5cm); female proportionately smaller. *Weight:* male 16–18lb (7–8kg); female 15–17lb (7–7.5kg).

Characteristics and Temperament
Bred for sporting pursuits, this is another big-hearted terrier. Fearless and ready for anything, the breed also makes an excellent family pet, joining in every game and always on the lookout for intruders.

The Wirehaired was developed in England by fox-hunting enthusiasts and is believed to be descended from a now-extinct rough-coated, black-and-tan working terrier used in Wales, Derbyshire, and Durham, where they were pulled out of foxholes by means of their docked tails.

GLEN OF IMAAL TERRIER

The breed gets its name from a glen in the Wicklow Mountains, Ireland. The Glen of Imaal Terrier only achieved recognition in 1930, the breed having been developed for digging into foxes' lairs and badger setts, its bowed front legs being considered an ideal adaptation. This is not a common breed, but its good nature and characterful appearance may well increase its appeal.

Appearance A tough-looking little dog, longish in the body and short of leg. The head has a fairly broad skull and a tapering muzzle. The nose is black. The brown eyes are set quite widely apart and are suggestive of intelligence. The small rose-shaped ears are half-pricked when alert but lowered when at rest. The strong neck is carried on a long body with a broad chest. The legs are short and strongly boned; the

front legs may be slightly bowed. The tail is often docked.

Coat Medium-length and coarse but with a soft undercoat. Colors are blue, wheaten and brindle.

Size *Height:* 14in (35.5cm). *Weight:* 35lb (16kg).

Characteristics and Temperament
This terrier, like most of its relatives, is alert and active and also likes water. It is gentle and affectionate with people.

In America the breed was fully recognized and entered the Terrier group in October 2004 through the efforts of members of the Glen of Imaal Terrier Club of America. There are now 500–600 Glens registered in the United States.

The popularity of the Irish Terrier quickly
extended to the USA and the Irish Terrier
Club of America was founded in 1896,
adopting the British standard for the breed; by
1929 it ranked 13th among the 79 breeds then
recognized by the AKC.

moderately long body with a straight,
strong back; the loins are muscular and
slightly arched. The legs are long with
plenty of muscle and bone. The tail is
usually docked to about three-quarters of
its length.

Coat Hard and wiry, with a broken
appearance. Colors are red, red-wheaten or
yellow-and-red.

Size *Height:* male 19in (48cm); female 18in
(46cm). *Weight:* 25–27lb (11–12kg).

Characteristics and Temperament
The breed has the reputation of being
something of a daredevil – rushing into
action without fear of the consequences. It
can be intolerant of other dogs, but with its
human companions it is the very model
of devotion, sensitivity, affection and
good nature.

IRISH TERRIER

The Irish Terrier, or Irish Red Terrier,
as it was once called, was first shown
in Ireland in the 1870s, although it had
been   used by sportsmen for many years
before that – and indeed still is. This was
the first Irish dog breed to be recognized by
the UK Kennel Club.

Appearance A wiry, racy-looking dog with
an attractive reddish coat. The head is long
with a flat, fairly narrow skull. The nose is
black. The eyes are dark and full of life.
The drop ears are small and V-shaped. The
neck is of a fair length and is carried on a

KERRY BLUE TERRIER

The Kerry Blue Terrier is believed to have originated in Kerry, Ireland, where it was originally used by farmers for hunting foxes, otters and badgers. Nowadays, however, with careful trimming to achieve the classic Kerry shape, it has been transformed into a successful show dog. In the 1920s, when the breed reached its peak, there were four clubs in Ireland devoted to the Kerry Blue, and where it was proclaimed 'well nigh faultless, if a slight tendency to demolish the cat population be excepted.'

Appearance A well-proportioned, muscular and upstanding dog. The long, lean head has strong, deep jaws and a fairly long muzzle. The nose is black. The eyes are small and dark and convey a typically keen terrier intelligence. The V-shaped drop ears are small. The neck is long and is carried on a short, deep-chested body. The legs are long and powerful, terminating in small feet. The tail, customarily docked, is carried erect.

Coat Profuse, soft and wavy. Color may be any shade of blue. Puppies are born black, and the color may take up to 18 months to develop.

Size *Height:* male 18–19in (46–48cm); female slightly less. *Weight:* male 33–37lb (15–17kg); female 35lb (16kg).

The Kerry's coat is the real point of interest in this breed. Some say the feature was introduced by a Portuguese Water Dog, which swam ashore from a shipwrecked vessel, possibly at the time of the Spanish Armada, when many vessels were lost on the rocks of south-west Ireland. Bedlington was later introduced, which would have reinforced the soft and silky quality of the coat and introduced the blue gene to help fix the color.

Characteristics and Temperament
This is an extroverted and determined dog, bred for the outdoor life and having many of the characteristics typical of terriers. Bold and game, the breed is also a good pet and house guard. Regular trimming is required to maintain the typical 'look.'

LAKELAND TERRIER

The Lakeland Terrier was developed in England's Lake District, its function being to run with the foxhunt. The UK Kennel Club formally recognized the breed in 1921. A popular show dog, one such dog achieved Best in Show at Crufts in 1967 and then went on to become Best in Show the following year at the American Westminster show. Regular careful grooming is needed to maintain the dog's classic appearance.

Appearance An attractive, compact and purposeful-looking dog. The head is flat and broad, with a medium to long muzzle. The nose is black, except in liver-colored dogs when it is also liver. Eyes are hazel or a darker shade of hazel. The ears are V-shaped and folded. The neck is slightly arched and carried on a shortish body with a strong back. The legs are long and powerful. The tail is customarily docked and carried high, but never over the back.

Coat Dense, hard and weatherproof. Colors are black-and-tan, blue-and-tan, wheaten, red, red grizzle, liver, blue, black.

Size *Height:* 14.5in (37cm). *Weight:* male 17lb (7.5kg); female 15lb (7kg).

The Lakeland Terrier sheds little to no hair automatically, but should have its coat plucked (stripped) two or three times each year, when the old hair should be pulled out by hand. Loose hair should also be removed from the ear passages and the excess hair between the pads of the feet trimmed away.

Characteristics and Temperament
Although small, the Lakeland Terrier is a tough, fearless and active dog, ever-alert and ready to work all day if necessary. The breed is also endearingly cheerful and affectionate, so that even when it is naughty it is not hard to forgive.

MANCHESTER TERRIER

Rat-catching contests were extremely popular in the north of England around the mid-1850s, and heavy wagers were placed on their outcome. This breed was developed for just such activities and soon gained the name of Manchester Terrier from the locality. The breed combined all the qualities required of such a sporting dog, including terrier instincts, a great turn of speed (there is a suggestion of Whippet in its ancestry) and a clean and easy manner in the home.

Appearance An attractive, clean-looking and smooth-coated dog. The head is long and wedge-shaped with a long, flat skull.

The small, almond-shaped eyes have a sparkle to them, and the small, V-shaped ears are carried above the topline of the head. The longish neck sits on a short, narrow body with slightly arched loins. Long and muscular legs end in semi-hare-like feet. The tail is fairly short and tapering to the tip.

Coat Short, close and glossy. Color is jet-black with rich tan, and precise placement of the tan markings is required.

Recollect that the Almighty, who gave the dog to be companion of our pleasures and our toils, hath invested him with a nature noble and incapable of deceit.

Sir Walter Scott

In the US, the Manchester Terrier is divided into two varieties, the Toy Manchester being the diminutive version of the standard Manchester Terrier. Apart from size and ear-type differences, both are identical.

Size *Height:* male 16in (40.5cm); female 15in (38cm). *Weight:* male 18lb (8kg); female 17lb (7.5kg).

Characteristics and Temperament
A graceful and elegant breed, the Manchester Terrier is a highly efficient rodent-catcher and general sporting dog. It also makes a devoted family pet, capable of fitting either into a town or country home; it is the ideal choice for a potential owner looking for something a little different.

NORFOLK TERRIER & NORWICH TERRIER

The Norfolk Terrier, and the almost identical Norwich Terrier, take their names from the English county of Norfolk and Norwich, Norfolk's county town. The breeds came about by crossing small red terriers with other terriers. Originally, there was no distinction between the Norfolk and the Norwich, but in 1964 it was decided that dogs with drop or folded ears should be called Norfolk Terriers and dogs with pricked ears should be classed Norwich Terriers. The AKC followed suit in 1979. The descriptions which follow apply to

According to the breed standard, Norfolks and Norwiches are self-confident little dogs that have a strong sense of presence and importance, holding their heads and tails proudly erect. A Norfolk or a Norwich that is shy, or carries its tail between its legs, is untypical, and suggests that it may be hot-tempered and aggressive toward other dogs.

the hair on the head and ears is shorter and smoother. Colors are red, wheaten, grizzle or black-and-tan.

Size *Height:* 10in (25.5cm). *Weight:* 10–12lb (4.5–5.5kg).

Characteristics and Temperament

These tough, energetic little dogs have occasionally been used to hunt badgers, foxes and rats. They love to dig and will continue digging and barking if left outside for long periods with nothing to occupy their active minds. Thoroughly fearless, they also make lovable, friendly pets.

both breeds, with the exception of the style of ears already described.

Appearance A small, compact and keen-looking dog. The head has a broad, slightly-rounded skull. The muzzle is wedge-shaped with a well-defined stop. The oval eyes are deep-set and either black or ßdark brown; they should have a keen and alert expression. The ears are medium-sized and pointed; in the Norfolk Terrier they are folded, and in the Norwich Terrier the ears are erect. A strong, medium-length neck is carried on a short, compact body. The legs are shortish but strong. The tail may be docked, but this is optional.

Coat The hard, straight and wiry coat is slightly longer on the neck and shoulders;

The Parson Russell is a dog of character, being intelligent, brave and at times even comical. It is equally at home in the show ring as it is in the home.

Coat The double coat must have a good sheen, whether it be smooth or broken, being naturally harsh, close, dense and straight, with no suggestion of a kink. Colors are all-white, or white with tan, lemon or black markings. Grizzle is acceptable but should not be confused with brindle, which attracts disqualification in show dogs.

Size *Height:* male 13–14in (33–35.5cm); female 13in (33cm). *Weight:* 14lb (6.5kg).

Characteristics and Temperament

A tough, active little worker, bred for pace and endurance, the Parson Jack Russell is a playful and intelligent rascal with sharp eyes and sharp wits. It makes a good house pet but can be destructive if left alone long enough to become bored.

PARSON JACK RUSSELL

The Parson Jack Russell Terrier gets its name from a Devonshire clergyman of that name. He was a Master of the Foxhounds who bred a small, active terrier using white-bodied Fox Terriers among other breeds. The dog has now achieved show status and comes in either smooth-coated or rough-coated forms. The Parson Russell described here is a longer-legged animal than the short-legged Jack Russell Terrier so commonly seen in farmyards and family homes in the UK. The Parson Russell Terrier was recognized by the UK Kennel Club in 1990, and by the American Kennel Club in 2001. On 1 April 2003, the AKC did something highly unusual: it changed a breed name. Officially 'Jack Russell' is now 'Parson Russell,' in keeping with the international standard set by the UK, the breed's place of origin.

Appearance Resembling a shorter-legged Fox Terrier, the head has a moderately broad and flat skull. The nose is black.

Keen, almond-shaped eyes produce an alert expression. Ears are V-shaped and folded. The neck is medium-length and muscular, carried on a body with a strong, straight back. Legs are muscular. The tail is straight and usually docked.

SCOTTISH TERRIER

A breed hailing from the Highlands of Scotland, the Scottish Terrier was originally used to destroy rodents and foxes. The standard for the breed was drawn up in 1880, and the Scottish Terrier Club was formed in 1882. Though still fairly popular, the Scottish Terrier is less commonly seen than it was about 50 years ago.

Appearance A sturdy, short-legged and thick-set dog, the head gives the impression of being large in comparison with the body-size. The head is long with a flat skull. The dark-brown eyes are deeply set beneath long eyebrows. The ears are finely pointed and pricked. A muscular neck is carried on a body with a deep chest and a short, muscular back. Short, strong legs terminate in good-sized feet. The tail is of moderate length and tapers at the tip.

Coat The outercoat is hard, dense and wiry, and the undercoat is short, soft and dense. Colors are black, wheaten or brindle.

Size *Height:* 10–11in (25.5–28cm). *Weight:* 19–23lb (8.5–10.5kg).

Characteristics and Temperament
At times somewhat reserved, the 'Scottie' is a vigilant and loyal companion. When it has a mind, it can move remarkably swiftly in pursuit of a toy such as a ball.

The Scottie is thought to be the oldest of the Highland terriers, although this has not been proved. What is certain is that Scotties and West Highland White Terriers are closely related, both their antecedents having originated in the Blackmount region of Perthshire and Rannoch Moor.

SEALYHAM

The Sealyham Terrier came about as the result of an obsession to produce the 'perfect terrier.' The person responsible for this undertaking was Captain John Edwardes of Haverfordwest in Pembrokeshire, Wales, who between 1850 and 1891 crossed a variety of terriers, namely Bull Terriers, Fox Terriers, West Highland Whites and others with Welsh Corgis to produce what became known as the Sealyham Terrier (*see opposite far left and below*). It was intended for hunting rats, foxes and badgers. Today's dog is somewhat different from the one envisaged by its creator, but it remains a versatile and an active breed.

Appearance A mobile, well-balanced dog of substance. The head has a broad, slightly-arched skull and a long, square muzzle. The nose is black, the round eyes are of medium size, and the ears are fairly large and folded. A long, thick and muscular neck is carried on a medium-length body with a deep, broad chest. The legs are short and strong and terminate in cat-like feet. The tail is short, customarily docked, and is carried erect.

Coat The outercoat is hard and wiry, with a weather-resistant undercoat. Colors are all-white, or white with brown, lemon, blue or pied markings on the ears and head. Heavy body markings and excessive ticking are considered incorrect.

The American Sealyham Terrier Club was founded on 15 May 1913 to promote the breed in the US and to encourage exhibitions and working trials. Today, however, the breed is distinctly rare and is considered by the UK Kennel Club to be one of Britain's most endangered native breeds.

Size *Height:* 12in (30.5cm). *Weight:* male 20lb (9kg); female 18lb (8kg).

Characteristics and Temperament
A faithful and intelligent little dog, the Sealyham is the perfect companion for both the town- and country-dweller. Excellent with children and always ready for play, it can usually find ways to amuse itself when its owner is busy.

SKYE TERRIER

Originally known as the Terrier of the Western Isles, the Skye Terrier gets its name from the Isle of Skye, in Scotland's Inner Hebrides. The dog was bred to hunt animals such as foxes, polecats, martens, otters and badgers. Most Skye Terriers have pricked ears, but there is also a variety that has drop ears.

Appearance A low, long dog with a very full coat. The head is long with a strong muzzle and a black nose. The eyes are close-set and dark-brown to hazel in color. The ears may be pricked or drop and are abundantly fringed with hair. The long neck is carried on a long, low body.

The legs are short. The tail is long and gracefully feathered.

Coat The highly characteristic outercoat is long, hard and straight, and the undercoat is woolly and soft. Colors are black, gray, cream or fawn, all with black points.

Size *Height:* 10in (25.5cm). *Weight:* 25lb (11kg).

Characteristics and Temperament This breed has the reputation of becoming strongly bonded and being faithful to one master, and can be wary of strangers. The Skye Terrier makes a good watchdog despite its size. The long, flowing coat needs regular grooming to keep it in first-class condition.

Greyfriars Bobby was a Skye Terrier in 19th-century Edinburgh, Scotland, which is said to have spent 14 years guarding its owner's grave until its own death in January 1872. Today, a small statue of the dog is located near Greyfriars Kirkyard.

SOFT-COATED WHEATEN TERRIER

An old breed of Irish terrier, the Soft-Coated Wheaten Terrier is very similar to the Kerry Blue in appearance and temperament. Indeed, they were both bred to perform similar tasks, hunting foxes, rats and badgers. The coat of the Wheaten Terrier may either be trimmed or left as it is. The breed was registered with the Kennel Club in Britain in 1943, and with the American Kennel Club in 1973.

As a pet, this terrier can get along with moderate but regular exercise.

Appearance A medium-sized, compact terrier with a soft, wheat-colored coat. The head is fairly long with a flat-topped skull and there is a well-defined stop. The nose is black. The eyes are dark hazel with dark eye-rims. The drop ears are V-shaped. The neck is moderately long, arched and muscular. A short and compact body is carried on strong, moderately long legs. The tail, customarily docked, is carried jauntily but never arched over the back.

Coat Soft and silky; curled or loosely waved. The coat is especially profuse on the head and legs. Color should be the color of wheat.

Size *Height:* male 18–19.5in (46–49.5cm); female slightly less. *Weight:* male 35–45lb (16–20.5kg); female slightly less.

Characteristics and Temperament
A natural sort of terrier with an extrovert and playful disposition, the dog is ready for action at any time. With patient training, the breed makes an excellent pet, being particularly good with children.

Our perfect companions never have fewer than four feet.

Colette

115

STAFFORDSHIRE BULL TERRIER

The result of crossings between Bulldogs and terriers, the breed was developed as a fighting dog, used for bull- and bear-baiting in Elizabethan England. When this cruel sport was abolished in the 19th century the dogs, by now having grown smaller and more agile, were pitted against each other instead. The name 'Staffordshire' comes from the breed's association with the Black Country region of England where it originated. Bull and terrier breeds are believed to have arrived in North America some time in the mid-1880s, where they developed along different lines, with heavier, taller dogs being the end result.

A PORTRAIT OF THE DOG

The Staffordshire Bull Terrier is related to the Bull Terrier and its larger cousins the American Staffordshire Terrier and the American Pit Bull Terrier, and is often categorized as a 'Pit Bull Terrier.' A breed standard was created and the Staffordshire was officially recognized by the UK Kennel Club in 1935.

Appearance A smooth-coated dog of muscular build and with a low center of gravity. The head is short and deep with a broad skull and prominent cheek muscles.

The nose is black. The round, medium-sized eyes are usually dark, but may vary according to coat-color. The ears are rose-shaped and half-pricked. A short, muscular neck is carried on a body with a broad chest and strong shoulders. The legs are well-boned and set widely apart. The tail is of medium length and carried rather low.

Coat Short, smooth and close-lying. Colors are red, fawn, white, black or blue, or any of these colors with white; also brindle or brindle-and-white.

Size *Height:* 14–16in (35.5–40.5cm). *Weight:* male 28–38lb (13–17kg); female 24–34lb (11–15kg).

Characteristics and Temperament
The breed's reputation as a pugnacious fighter indicates that it needs careful training and firm handling when in the vicinity of other dogs. With people, however, the Staffie is affectionate and calm and good with children. The dog is naturally brave, strong and fiercely tenacious but also has a lively intelligence.

WELSH TERRIER

The Welsh Terrier was originally used for hunting badgers, foxes and otters. Its devotees say it resembles a smaller version of the Airedale Terrier (which it certainly resembles color-wise), although it is more likely that it shares a common ancestry with the Lakeland Terrier. It was introduced to America in the 1880s.

Appearance A squarely-built, workmanlike dog with a smart appearance. The head has a flat, moderately narrow skull and a longish muzzle. The nose is black. The eyes are small and dark and suggest courage.

The drop ears are small and triangular. The neck is long and slightly arched and is carried on a short body with strong loins. The legs are moderately long and well-boned. The tail is docked and carried with a jaunty air.

Coat Profuse, dense and wiry; a double coat is preferred. Colors are black-and-tan, although black, grizzle-and-tan is also permitted.

Size *Height:* 15.5in (39.5cm). *Weight:* 20–21lb (9–9.5kg).

Characteristics and Temperament
The Welsh Terrier has the typical, terrier 'tip-toe' stance, suggesting it is ready for anything. A good worker, the breed also makes a clever and happy companion for the house, being far from shy, always affectionate, and usually obedient.

Recognized as a breed since 1886, the Welsh Terrier probably stemmed from an British black-and-tan terrier that existed as early as the 13th century.

The breed was first shown at Crufts in London in 1907. In 1908 it was registered as the Roseneath Terrier with the AKC, the name being officially changed to the West Highland White Terrier on 31 May 1909.

strong loins. The legs are short and strong. The tail should be as straight as possible and carried jauntily.

Coat The outercoat is harsh, long and with no curl; the undercoat is short, soft and close. Color should be pure white.

Size *Height:* 11in (28cm). *Weight:* male 19lb (8.5kg); female 16.5lb (7.5kg).

Characteristics and Temperament
The 'Westie' is a deservedly popular little dog, possessing a lively and outgoing personality; it is always ready for a game and seems to have boundless energy. A sharp bark to warn off strangers also makes it a useful guard dog.

WEST HIGHLAND WHITE

The breed is thought to have originated in Poltalloch, Scotland, where the Malcolm family bred these white terriers for several generations. In fact, the dogs were originally called Poltalloch Terriers. These smart little sporting dogs are also much admired in the show ring and as companions.

Appearance An eager, squarely-built little terrier with a characteristic white coat. The head has a slightly arched skull with a tapering muzzle and a black nose. The medium-sized eyes are set widely apart; the color should be as dark as possible, producing the piercing look. The ears are small, erect and pointed. The body is compact, with a deep chest and broad,

CHAPTER FOUR
UTILITY DOGS

The utility, or non-sporting, group includes dogs of many different shapes and sizes performing a variety of tasks. The group ranges from the large breeds, such as the Japanese Akita and the Leonberger, to the much smaller oriental breeds like the Shih Tzu. The group is sometimes said to include all the breeds that do not satisfactorily fit into any of the other main categories. However, a more useful criterion for classification might be that within the utility group are to be found dogs that are appreciated first and foremost for their companionship, but which may also undertake other useful roles such as guarding property. (This does not mean, however, that dogs from some of the other groups are not efficient guards or do not make good companions.)

All the breeds found within the utility group, however, seem to have an hereditary aptitude for defending and guarding. Some, like the Bulldog and the Japanese Akita, were originally bred as fighting dogs, and these aggressive qualities stood them in good stead when they were required to stand guard. Even among the breeds which did not display these gladiatorial skills, there is a propensity to give voice in no uncertain manner at the arrival of strangers to the door, making such animals ideal watchdogs. This is a virtue no less important today than in the past, for it is a well-known fact that a property guarded by a loudly barking dog is a much less attractive proposition for a would-be burglar than one in which the arrival of a stranger is greeted by silence. Although the

OPPOSITE BELOW: The Leonberger never seems to be in a hurry, but is happy to amble along at its own pace. Unusually, it has webbed feet, making it an excellent swimmer.

RIGHT: Poodles are intelligent creatures, once highly prized as performing animals in circuses and stage shows due to their ability to quickly learn new tricks. The Toy and Miniatures are most suited to the town, whereas the Standard Poodle, shown here, is a true country dog at heart.

modern-day utility dog is not usually pugnacious by nature, most will be prepared to respond appropriately if there is a real threat to the family or home that they believe they are guarding.

Among the diverse shapes and sizes to be found within the utility group, there are some that are fairly uniform in type and appearance. These are the Spitz breeds, which are of Arctic origin; these hardy animals were bred to work in the harsh and inhospitable conditions of the frozen north. They all have compact, muscular bodies and loud voices. Among the adaptations designed to help reduce heat loss from the body are thick, insulating coats, hooded ears, and tails that are usually held curled over the back, close to the body. Spitz dogs were, and in some places still are, expected to carry out a wide range of tasks. These include guarding domestic herds, working as watchdogs, hunting, and acting as draft dogs – pulling sleds or carrying tents and other equipment on their backs. They probably also served a useful function by being something warm to sleep next to on a cold night.

Another group of utility dogs, the Schnauzers, are sometimes called German terriers. They do not bark with the frequency that characterizes Spitz dogs, but

are generally considered to be more intelligent. The larger versions of Schnauzers, in particular, can be rather willful unless trained correctly to bring out their best qualities and character. They also need to be handled correctly to prevent them from trying to get the upper hand.

Some of the other dogs within the utility group can also be trained to perform

useful tasks over and above those of guard or companion. The Dalmatian, a keen and powerful runner, can be trained for hunting and retrieving, while Poodles, too, have considerable retrieving skills, and are particularly adept at gathering fallen birds from water; they are also sometimes used to sniff out truffles lying buried beneath the ground.

BOSTON TERRIER

A true American creation, resulting from a cross between an English Bulldog and a white English terrier. In about 1870 William O'Brien of Boston sold an imported dog, named Judge, to Robert C. Hooper, also of Boston. This dog was commonly known as 'Hooper's Judge' and was the ancestor of nearly all of today's true Boston Terriers.

Appearance A muscular dog with distinctive, erect ears, an alert expression, and a striking coat. The head is square-shaped with a short, wide muzzle. The nose is black. The large, round eyes are set widely apart. The ears are carried erect.

The Boston Terrier was recognized by the American Kennel Club in 1893, making its first appearance in the UK in the 1920s.

The slightly arched neck is carried on a short, deep-chested body. The legs are strong and muscular and the tail is short.

Coat Short and glossy. Brindle-and-white are the preferred colors, but black-and-white is also permissible. The breed standard describes how the white content of the coat should ideally be distributed.

Size *Height:* 15–17in (38–43cm). *Weight:* not to exceed 25lb (11.5kg). Divided into classes as follows: under 15lb (7kg); 15–20lb (7–9kg); and 20–25lb (9–11.5kg).

Characteristics and Temperament
A dapper, small to medium-sized dog, strong-willed and determined but nevertheless amiable and intelligent.

BULLDOG

One of the most instantly recognizable of dogs, the Bulldog is the national dog of Britain and is known the world over as a symbol of indomitable spirit and determination. The history of the Bulldog probably goes back to at least the 1600s, when it was used for bull-baiting and dog fights (the shape of its jaws meant it could grab bulls' noses and hang on). Fortunately this and similar barbaric pursuits were abolished in the 19th century, when the dog became a show dog and companion, the ferocity of earlier individuals having been bred out.

Appearance A massively-built, low and sturdy dog. The head is massive and deep with a broad, square skull and a short,

broad muzzle with an upturned lower jaw. The nose is black. The eyes are round, set widely apart, and have a quizzical and appealing look. The rose ears are small. The neck is thick, deep and powerful. The body is short, broad in front and narrow toward the rear; the chest is deep and broad. The fore legs are stout and planted far apart; they can appear slightly bowed, although the bones themselves are actually straight; the hind legs are longer. The tail is rather short and tapers to a fine point.

Coat Fine, short and close. Coat-color must be uniform, pure of its kind, and brilliant. The various colors are listed here in order of preference: red brindle, all other brindles, solid white, solid red, fawn or fallow, piebald; the least favored are

Bulldogs have extremely strong jaws, and are said to be capable of suspending themselves from objects for long periods, using their vice-like grip.

inferior versions of the foregoing. However, a perfect piebald is preferable to a muddy brindle or defective solid color. Solid black is undesirable, but not if it occurs to a moderate degree in piebald patches.

Size *Height:* 12–14in (30.5–36cm). *Weight:* male 55lb (25kg); female 50lb (22.5kg).

Characteristics and Temperament
The Bulldog's pugilistic appearance belies an affectionate nature. Somewhat stubborn and tenacious on occasions, the breed is nevertheless good with children and is a protective watchdog when required. The Bulldog can also be said to be humorous – even comical – which adds to its charm. Would-be owners should note that, although the Bulldog has a good turn of speed when needed, it usually prefers to proceed at a more leisurely pace. Due to the shape of its breathing apparatus, it can become short of breath if overexerted.

If you eliminate smoking and gambling, you will be amazed to find that almost all an Englishman's pleasures can be, and mostly are, shared by his dog.

George Bernard Shaw

127

CANAAN DOG

This is the national dog of Israel. It was selectively bred from pariah dogs, the feral or semi-wild dogs common in parts of North Africa and countries of the Middle East and Asia. This is a comparatively rare breed outside its native land.

Appearance A medium-sized, well-balanced dog. The wedge-shaped head has a fairly flat skull and a moderately broad muzzle. The nose is black. The almond-shaped eyes are dark. The prominent ears are erect and broad at the base. The body is square, with a level back and muscular loins. The legs are long and strong and end

Canaan Dogs once guarded the flocks of the ancient Israelites, but as the Hebrew population diminished, most of them sought refuge in the Negev Desert, a natural reservoir of Israeli wildlife. Avoiding extinction, they remained undomesticated for the most part, although some lived with the Bedouins, earning their keep by guarding their camps.

in round, cat-like feet. The tail is long and bushy, and is held curled over the back when on the move.

Coat Straight, hard and of medium length. Colors are sandy to tan, black, white or spotted; white markings are permissible in all coat-colors.

Size *Height:* 20–24in (51–61cm). *Weight:* 40–55lb (18–25kg).

Characteristics and Temperament
Alert and intelligent, the Canaan Dog can be rather aloof with strangers but makes a good watchdog. In movement, the dog moves with athletic agility and grace, using a brisk, ground-covering trot.

CHOW CHOW

A Spitz-type dog that has been known in China for about 2,000 years. The true origin of the Chow Chow is unknown, but the breed, as it is known today, is easily recognizable from artefacts of the Han Dynasty (206 BC–AD 220). An all-purpose dog, it was used for hunting, herding and protecting the home. Some claim it was the ancestor of the Samoyed, Norwegian Elkhound, Pomeranian and Keeshond. Because China was closed to outsiders for long periods in its history, the breed did not appear in other countries until the 1800s.

There are two types of Chow Chow: smooth-coated and rough-coated.

Appearance A heavy-looking, woolly-coated dog with a leonine appearance. The head has a heavy, broad skull and a medium-length, broad muzzle. The nose is black, while the gums, roof of mouth and tongue are blue-black. The eyes are dark and oval-shaped, and the ears are small and pricked. A strong neck is carried on a short, broad, deep-chested body. The legs are heavily-boned and muscular. The tail is carried curled over the back.

Coat Rough-coated dogs have a coat that is thick and abundant; the outercoat is somewhat coarse and the undercoat is soft and woolly; it is especially thick around the neck and behind the legs. In smooth-coated dogs the coat is short, dense, straight and plush. Colors are solid black, red, blue, cream, fawn or white.

Size *Height:* male 19–22in (48–56cm); female 18–20in (46–51cm). *Weight:* 55lb (25kg).

Characteristics and Temperament
In general, the Chow Chow does not take readily to strangers, and because of its deep-set eyes is best approached from the front. Rather independent, and seldom moving at any great speed, this is a quiet dog that may not appeal to everyone.

The Chow Chow is most commonly kept as a companion dog today, although its keen sense of ownership of the home, paired with a sometimes disconcerting approach to strangers, can be off-putting to those unfamiliar with the breed. Chows are not a particularly active breed, so life in an apartment could suit them well, provided time is set aside each day for a brisk walk.

DALMATIAN

A breed that is recognizable by anyone with a passing interest in dogs, the Dalmatian was highly popular in Britain during the Regency period between 1795 and 1837. Then it was also known as the 'carriage dog,' since it was accustomed to run alongside or even beneath all kinds of carriages. In both Britain and America it also used to run in front of horse-drawn fire engines. The ability to run in such a way was possible because of the great stamina and endurance possessed by the breed. Today, the Dalmatian is a popular, friendly and long-lived pet.

Appearance A clean-looking, elegant and athletic dog with a distinctive coat pattern. The head is fairly long, with a broad skull and a long, strong muzzle. The nose is black in black-spotted varieties and brown in liver-spotted individuals. The eyes are dark or amber, according to the coat-color; they should look bright and express intelligence. The ears are fairly large and pendulous. A long, well-arched neck is carried on a deep-chested body with a powerful back. The legs are long and muscular. The tail is long and carried with a slight upward curve when the dog is on the move.

Coat Short, dense, glossy and sleek. The ground color is pure white, evenly covered with either black or liver spots.

Size *Height:* male 23–24in (58.5–61cm); female 22–23in (56–58.5cm). *Weight:* male 55lb (25kg); female 49.5lb (22kg).

The Dalmatian's heritage is hotly disputed, although no definite conclusions have yet been reached. Contrary to popular belief, there is no evidence that the breed originated in Dalmatia (Croatia), but it is certainly a dog of ancient lineage that has survived the centuries virtually unchanged. Images of dogs resembling Dalmatians, running alongside chariots, have been discovered in Egyptian tombs.

Characteristics and Temperament
The Dalmatian has great freedom of movement, using a long-striding, rhythmic action to cover the ground. A good sporting dog if required – with boundless energy and enthusiasm – the breed is also the perfect house dog and companion for an active family.

FRENCH BULLDOG

Lace-makers from England working in France in the 1850s took their small Bulldogs with them, and it is thought that these bred with local French dogs to produce the French Bulldog. The French Bulldog was introduced to Britain in the early part of the 20th century.

Appearance A small, sturdy and compact dog with characteristic 'bat' ears. The head is square, with a broad, short skull and muzzle. The nose is black. The eyes are round and set forward, giving the dog an expression of trust. The bat ears are wide at the base and held upright and parallel. The powerful neck is carried on a short and muscular body with a deep chest. The legs are short and powerful, the hind legs being longer than the front legs. The tail is short and thick at the root.

Coat Short, close, glossy and smooth. Colors are brindle, pied or fawn.

Size *Height:* 12–12.5in (30.5–32cm). *Weight:* 24–28lb (11–13kg).

Characteristics and Temperament
Like the British Bulldog, breathing can be somewhat restricted in the French dog, therefore it may be inclined to take things at its own pace from time to time – although it can rush about well enough when the need arises. This is a jolly, affectionate and endearing breed which is quiet in the house and only too happy to curl up with family and friends.

The French Bulldog is easy to groom using a rubber grooming mitt, that will remove loose and dead hair. The deep face-wrinkles should be checked from time to time and cleaned if necessary.

GERMAN SPITZ

In Germany, there are five different varieties of Spitz dogs, ranging in size from the large Wolfspitz to the small Pomeranian. The two varieties described here are the *klein* (small) and the *mittel* (medium) varieties, and apart from the difference in size the two are identical. The Wolfspitz is also referred to as the Keeshond, but is recognized as a separate breed by the Kennel Club of Great Britain and other registries.

Appearance A compact, full-coated dog with erect ears. The head has a broad, flattish skull with the muzzle narrowing to a wedge. The nose is either black or a color harmonizing with the coat. The eyes are dark, either black or a tone harmonizing

with the coat. The small ears are held completely erect. The body is short with well-developed loins. The legs are well-boned and terminate in cat-like feet. The tail is held curled up over the back.

Coat The opulent double coat consists of a long, hard, straight outercoat and a soft, woolly undercoat. The fur is very thick around the neck and forequarters. All colors are acceptable, including chocolate, white and fawn.

Size *Height:* small 9–11.5in (23–29cm); medium 12–15in (30–38cm). *Weight:* small 17.5–22lb (8–10kg); medium 23–25lb (10.5–11.5kg).

Characteristics and Temperament
Cheerful and friendly and showing no signs of nervousness or aggression, and with an undemanding appetite, the German Spitz enjoys family life. Its long coat keeps it warm in the coldest weather, but requires regular and thorough grooming.

The German Spitz is a direct descendant of Arctic or Nordic herding dogs, such as the Samoyed, which were probably taken to Germany and Holland by Vikings during the Middle Ages, spreading throughout Europe where they were crossed with other herding and shepherd breeds, thus laying the foundation of the ubiquitous Spitz type.

KEESHOND

The Keeshond takes its name from the Dutch patriot Cornelius de Gyselaer, whose nickname was 'Kees.' The dog was adopted as a mascot in the years before the French Revolution, although it already had long associations as a watchdog for Dutch bargemen and is still known as the Dutch Barge Dog. The dog's popularity declined somewhat in the years leading up to 1920, but was revived through the efforts of Baroness von Hardenbroek, who bred some fine examples. Today, the breed's excellent guarding instincts are still utilized, and the dog is also a popular family companion.

Appearance A compact, Spitz dog with a bushy coat. The fox-like head has a moderately broad skull and a narrowing muzzle. The nose is black. The eyes are dark and almond-shaped. The small triangular ears are held erect. The neck is moderately long and arched, and is carried on a short and compact body. The legs are strongly muscled and terminate in cat-like feet. The tail is of moderate length and is held curled tightly over the back.

Coat The outercoat is harsh, straight and stand-off, and there is a short, thick, soft undercoat. The coat forms a dense ruff around the neck as well as providing ample feathering on the legs above the hocks. Coat-color is a mixture of black and gray.

Size *Height:* male 18in (46cm); female 17in (43cm). *Weight:* 43lb (19.5kg).

The Keeshond was accepted for registration by the American Kennel Club in 1930, and early development in that country, with few exceptions, was based on imports coming from Holland and Germany via England.

138

Characteristics and Temperament
This is a delightful, trusting and cheerful breed, good with children and always ready for exercise. Alert to every sound, the breed makes an excellent watchdog. The thick coat means that the Keeshond is happy to be out in even the coldest weather. Thorough grooming should be carried out very regularly.

LEONBERGER

This very substantial dog, the result of crossing St. Bernards with Newfoundlands, comes from Leonberg in Germany, where in 1840 the mayor decided to create a new breed in honor of the town. An even-tempered and intelligent dog, the breed was nevertheless in serious decline, following both World Wars, but in due course the few remaining specimens were used to re-establish the breed.

Appearance A large, purposeful-looking dog with a medium-length coat. The head has a fairly wide skull and a broad, square muzzle. The dark eyes have a friendly, intelligent expression. The pendulous ears are well-feathered and have rounded tips. The strong neck is carried on a deep-chested body. The legs are well-boned, strong and muscular, terminating in webbed feet. The tail is long and carried 'at half mast.'

Coat The coat is medium-length and varies in texture from fairly soft to hard; it may be wavy, but should on no account be curly. Colors are yellow or golden to red-brown, preferably with a black mask.

Size *Height:* male 28–32in (71–81cm); female 26–30in (66–76cm). *Weight:* 75–110lb (34–50kg).

Popular legend has it that the Leonberger was bred to resemble the lion on Leonberg's coat-of-arms, but in fact the earliest Leonbergers were predominantly white, the coloring of today's dogs – brownish with black masks – having been developed later in the 19th century, probably by introducing other breeds.

Characteristics and Temperament
The Leonberger never seems to be in a hurry, happy to amble along at its own speed. An easy-going, friendly dog, it can nevertheless give a good account of itself when called upon to guard the household. The breed likes the outdoor life and is a keen swimmer, as suggested by its webbed feet. The Leonberger has a hearty appetite.

LHASA APSO

This little dog originated in Tibet, where it was used as a watchdog in monasteries to alert the monks to the presence of intruders. Many of these dogs lived at high altitudes in the mountains, and the breed's long coat and warm undercoat, together with the generous covering of hair over the face, helped keep it warm. Apsos first appeared in Britain in the 1920s.

Appearance A solid dog with a long coat. The head has a medium-to-narrow skull and a blunt muzzle. The nose is black. The oval eyes are dark brown. The pendulous ears have a very generous covering of hair. A long neck is carried on a long, deep-chested body. The legs are short, terminating in cat-like feet. The tail is carried curled over the back.

Coat The outercoat is long, straight and hard; the undercoat is dense. Colors range from golden, sandy, honey, grizzle, slate, smoke, parti-color, black, white and brown.

Size *Height:* male 10in (25.5cm); female slightly smaller. *Weight:* 13–15.5lb (6–7kg).

Characteristics and Temperament
The Lhasa Apso is alert and watchful. Strangers are likely to be greeted with penetrating barking, that belies the dog's size. But as a family dog the breed is affectionate and cheerful, and hardy enough to be taken for long walks. The coat needs regular careful grooming to avoid it becoming hopelessly matted.

The American Kennel Club officially accepted the Lhasa Apso into the Terrier group in 1935, but transferred it to the Non-Sporting group in 1959.

MINIATURE SCHNAUZER

This bright and lively German dog is believed to have originated as a result of crossing a Standard Schnauzer with an Affenpinscher or Poodle. The Miniature Schnauzer closely resembles a terrier in appearance and character – and indeed, in America, it is placed within that group. Schnauzers also come in a Giant form, also stemming from the Standard Schnauzer.

Appearance A sturdy, alert-looking dog of nearly square proportions. The head is long with a flat skull and strong muzzle. The nose is black. The dark eyes are oval and set forward in the skull. The V-shaped ears are usually folded forward, although in some countries they are cropped. The arched, moderately-long neck is carried on a short body with a fairly deep chest. The legs are well-boned and muscular. The tail is usually docked.

Coat Rough and wiry, with a bushy beard and eyebrows. Colors are pure black, black-and-silver, or all pepper-and-salt (dark gray).

Size *Height:* male 14in (35.5cm); female 13in (33cm). *Weight:* male 20lb (9kg); female 16.5lb (7.5kg).

Characteristics and Temperament
Adaptable, alert and fast-moving, this breed is the ideal companion – whether it be for an active family looking for a dog to share its home or an older person looking for a trusted and loyal friend.

The Miniature Schnauzer was recognized by the US United Kennel Club in 1948, but the UK does not accept it as a true terrier because it does not originate from the classic terrier breeds of the British Isles.

POODLE

The Poodle comes in three sizes: Toy, Miniature and Standard. It is one of the most recognizable of breeds, due to the fact that its fur is often clipped into very distinctive shapes. Despite the somewhat unlikely appearance of some show poodles, the breed was originally used as a truffle-hunter and as a retriever, being especially adept at gathering from water. Although considered a French dog, it is more likely that it originated in Germany and was later taken to France. In some countries the Toy Poodle is placed in the Toy group.

Appearance An elegant-looking and balanced dog with a distinctive coat. The head is long with a moderately broad skull and a strong muzzle. The almond-shaped eyes are black or dark brown, and express great intelligence and spirit. The ears are long and hang close to the face. The neck is strong and carries the head with dignity. The body is broad and deep-chested with powerful loins. The legs are long and well-boned. The tail is usually docked and is carried away from the body at a slight angle.

While parti-colored Poodles cannot be shown in the American Kennel Club, Canadian Kennel Club, or any Fédération Cynologique Internationale conformation ring, they can be shown in the UK Kennel Club show ring and in all performance rings in Britain.

Coat Dense and profuse with a harsh texture; the coat does not molt (of interest to people normally allergic to dogs); it is often clipped into patterns such as the Lion clip or the less fussy Dutch clip. Poodles come in a variety of solid colors, including white, black, apricot and gray, but never parti-colored.

Size *Height:* Toy under 11in (28cm); Miniature 11–15in (28–38cm); Standard over 15in (38cm). *Weight:* Toy 10lb (4.5kg); Miniature 13lb (6kg); Standard 66–75lb (30–34kg).

Characteristics and Temperament
Poodles are intelligent dogs, once highly prized as performing animals in circuses and theaters due to their ability to learn quickly. The two smaller breeds are the most suited to a life in town, whereas the Standard is a country dog at heart. All Poodles, however, are friendly, high-spirited dogs and make good pets.

SCHNAUZER

The Schnauzer, also known as the Standard Schnauzer, is the original breed of the three types of Schnauzer, and despite its wiry coat and general appearance, is not related to the British terriers. A German breed with a long history, the dog was historically used for ratting, herding livestock, pulling carts and guarding property.

Appearance A robust, almost square dog with an alert manner. The head has a rather broad skull and a fairly long, strong muzzle. The nose is black. The eyes are oval and dark. The V-shaped ears usually drop forward but are cropped in some countries. The neck is strong and slightly arched and is carried on a short body with a moderately deep chest. The legs are muscular and well-developed, terminating in cat-like feet. The tail is usually docked.

Coat Wiry, harsh and short with a dense undercoat; prominent mustache, whiskers and eyebrows. Colors are either pure black or pepper-and-salt (shades of gray).

Size *Height:* male 19in (48cm); female 18in (46cm). *Weight:* male 39.5lb (18kg); female 35lb (16kg).

This Schnauzer has been used in various roles in modern times: by the Red Cross for guard duty during the First World War, and at one time or another by German and American police departments. They have also been used in the US for drug and bomb detection, and also in search-and-rescue.

Characteristics and Temperament
An outgoing and lively dog with a trustworthy nature, the Schnauzer actually looks fiercer than it actually is, although this stands it in good stead when called upon to guard property. Fond of children and always ready for work or play, the Schnauzer makes an ideal companion.

The Shar Pei is not to everyone's taste, although it has its fair share of enthusiastic admirers. It needs plenty of attention if skin problems are to be avoided.

raised beneath the loins. The legs are muscular and strong. The tail tapers at the tip and may be carried high and curved or curled over the back.

Coat Bristly, short and hard and standing off from the body. Colors are solid black, red, cream or fawn.

Size *Height:* 18–20in (46–51cm). *Weight:* 35–44lb (16–20kg).

Characteristics and Temperament
This is a vigorous and active dog. Early exports were reported to have some physical and temperamental problems, but the breed has been vastly improved over the last few decades.

SHAR PEI

A Chinese breed, the Shar Pei was originally bred for use as a guard, hunter and herding dog. This is a most unusual-looking dog, with a suggestion of Mastiff in its ancestry. Early examples in the West were short in the leg and unfortunately tended to suffer from a condition known as *entropion* (inward rolling of the eyelid), but the breed has become greatly improved in recent years. Devotees of the breed will not hear a word said against it, although others will find its appearance not to their liking.

Appearance A squarely-built dog with a characteristically wrinkled skin and frowning expression. The head is rather large and rectangular, and the muzzle is long, broad and padded. The nose is preferably black, but any color harmonizing with the coat-color is permitted. The eyes are almond-shaped and may be dark or light, depending on the coat-color. The ears are small, triangular and folded. The neck is short and strong. The body is short and deep and slightly

SHIH TZU

The Shih Tzu comes originally from Tibet, although it was developed in China and found favor at the royal courts of the imperial palaces. Records dating to AD 624 show dogs very similar to the Shih Tzu being given as tributes to the Tang emperor. The name Shih Tzu translates as 'lion dog,' and is believed to be a reference to the dog's pluckiness rather than to its appearance. The first examples of the breed were seen in Britain in 1931. In North America, the breed is placed in the Toy group rather than the Utility.

Appearance A long-coated little dog with a proud carriage. The head is broad and round with a short, square muzzle. The nose is usually black but may be liver-colored in liver or liver-marked dogs. The eyes are large, round and dark and have a

The Shih Tzu was admitted for registration in the American Kennel Club Stud Book in March 1969 and to regular AKC show classification in the Toy group, beginning in September 1969.

friendly expression. The ears are large and pendulous. The body is long with a deep chest. The legs are short, muscular and well-boned. The well-plumed tail is carried curled over the back.

Coat Long, straight and dense, with a dense undercoat; a slight wave is permitted in the coat, but not a curl; the facial hair should form a good beard and whiskers, and hair growing upward over the nose-bridge should create the familiar 'chrysanthemum' look. All colors are permitted.

Size *Height:* male 10.5in (27cm); female 9in (23cm). *Weight:* 10–16lb (4.5–7kg).

Characteristics and Temperament
An outgoing, enthusiastic little dog, the Shih Tzu is also intelligent and friendly and makes a good family addition. Moderate exercise is all that is required, but regular grooming is needed to keep the coat glossy and tangle-free.

TIBETAN SPANIEL

Bred in the border valleys between Tibet and China, this was one of the first Tibetan breeds to reach Britain, arriving in about 1900. In its native land it was popular among members of the royal courts as well as in monasteries.

Appearance A neat little dog, with a head that is slightly small compared with the body; the head is slightly domed, with a shortish muzzle. The nose is usually black. The dark-brown, oval eyes are of medium size and are set widely apart but forward-looking. The medium-sized ears are pendulous. The neck is short and strong, carried on a longish body with a good chest and level back. The legs are moderately boned, the fore legs being slightly bowed; the legs terminate in hare-like feet. The plumed tail is held curled over the back.

Coat A silky outercoat; smooth on face and front of legs; undercoat dense and fine. All colors are permitted.

Size *Height:* 10in (25.5cm). *Weight:* 9–15lb (4–7kg).

Characteristics and Temperament Another of the small and dignified oriental breeds, the Tibetan Spaniel is nevertheless far from staid and enjoys mad moments racing around outside. Somewhat aloof with strangers, it is intelligent, loyal and a good watchdog.

The Tibetan Spaniel has a shared ancestry with the Pekingese, Japanese Chin, Shih Tzu, Lhasa Apso, and Pug. It is not a true spaniel and may have been given the name due to its passing resemblance to the Cavalier King Charles Spaniel.

TIBETAN TERRIER

The Tibetan Terrier has a history going back over 2,000 years, and recent DNA analysis would seem to bear this out. In its native land it was thought to bring luck to its owner as well as having religious associations, being also known as the Holy Dog. Although they are called terriers, they are in fact herding dogs, and were often used to accompany traders traveling to and from China.

Appearance A well-built, long-coated dog reminiscent of a small Old English Sheepdog. The head has a medium-length skull and a strong muzzle. The nose is black. The round, dark-brown eyes are large and set widely apart. The V-shaped ears are pendent and heavily feathered. The neck is of medium length, carried on a compact, well-muscled body. The legs are well-boned, terminating in large, round feet. The well-plumed tail is carried curled over the back.

Coat The outercoat is profuse, fine and long, straight or waved, but not curled; the undercoat is fine and woolly. Colors are white, cream, gold, smoke, gray, black, parti-color or tricolor.

The Tibetian Terrier is bursting with energy, and requires regular play sessions to maintain its zest for life.

Size *Height:* male 14–16in (35.5–40.5cm); female slightly smaller. *Weight:* 18–31lb (8–14kg).

Characteristics and Temperament
The largest of the Tibetan breeds in the Utility group. An energetic and enthusiastic dog, the Tibetan Terrier is friendly to those it knows, loyal and full of character. The dog makes a good pet and is protective of its family.

CHAPTER FIVE
WORKING DOGS

This group of dogs includes more breeds than any other. In some countries, this large group is split into two smaller ones: working dogs and herding dogs. The Working Dogs group features breeds that, between them, do a variety of work, such as guarding, herding, carrying loads or pulling sleds and other vehicles, law enforcement duties, and rescue work. Some are bred to do more than one task: thus, for example, the Alaskan Malamute is a powerful sled-pulling dog, but its huge size and loud bark mean that it also performs an important role as a guard dog.

In addition to these roles, many of the dogs in this group are among the most popular as companions and pets.

This group has within it animals of hugely differing shapes and dimensions. They range in size from the small Welsh Corgi, standing only 10–12in (25.5–30.5cm) high, to the giant of the group – the Anatolian Shepherd Dog at 32in (81cm). But although this huge dog is the tallest of the group, it is not the heaviest; the Mastiff can weigh up to 190lb (86kg). Despite any differences in vital statistics, what these dogs all have in common is generation upon generation of breeding that has brought them to the peak of perfection for their purpose. Each dog, whatever its size, is ideally suited to the task expected of it, and many are indispensable servants of mankind. Most also share common traits of intelligence and obedience, as well as an inbuilt compulsion to do the job for which they were bred.

The history of herding dogs goes back thousands of years, when nomadic tribes adopted mountain dogs to act as guards, both to protect their herds from marauding wolves, bears and other predators, and to act as watchdogs against thieves and other enemies. Thus the dogs had to be big, strong and courageous. Interestingly, light-colored or even white dogs were favored, since they could more easily be distinguished from attackers at night. The majority of these dogs carried Mastiff blood, which no doubt gave them the fighting qualities so necessary for them to do their work. Among the best-known examples of these are the Estrela Mountain Dog, the Hungarian Kuvasz and the Pyrenean Mountain Dog.

Later, as some of these mountain tribes began to settle in the fertile valleys and lowlands, the need for such large and often cumbersome dogs began to diminish. The requirement was now for smaller, faster and more mobile dogs that could keep large

Keen, alert and responsive, hard-working and intelligent – these are only some of the attributes that have made the Border Collie such a successful working dog.

flocks of domestic animals together in one place. Many of these dogs became the ancestors of modern-day sheepdogs, such as the various types of collies, as well as the quick-moving Australian Cattle Dog and the Lancashire Heeler. Some of the world's working sheepdogs are hardly ever seen outside their native lands, and the qualities that suit them for a life spent working with livestock do not always translate into suitable attributes for the show ring or even family life.

The qualities required of a herding dog include the ability to control large flocks of cattle, sheep, goats or other livestock and to quickly and obediently respond to the commands of the shepherd. It is also vital that the dogs are instinctively protective toward their owner and the animals in their charge. These traits, together with a high degree of intelligence and willingness to be trained, mean that dogs of this type also make excellent guard dogs. This is not to say that training is always a simple task, however. Many of these breeds are strong-minded – and strong-bodied – dogs that need some initial convincing that their owners' bidding is the best course of action for them!

Among the working dogs whose role was primarily to guard property and people are included the Boxer, the Bullmastiff, the Dobermann and the German Shepherd Dog (often more commonly known as the Alsatian). These are all strong, active dogs with highly developed protective instincts. Although this quality is one of their main virtues, it must not be allowed to develop to the extent that the dog becomes over-protective and aggressive. Difficult behavior in such large and potentially dangerous dogs can be a real problem, and ownership of such breeds must be considered carefully, with correct training and handling adhered to at all times. It is vital

that dogs such as these are fully aware of their place in the 'pack' and respond quickly and consistently to commands from their owner.

The intelligent German Shepherd Dog is one of several working dogs that is so versatile that it can be utilized in a variety of different roles. As its name suggests, the breed was initially developed as a watchful herding dog, but it has found favor the world over in roles that include being police dogs, sniffer dogs (for drugs, explosives and

people buried under collapsed buildings), guard dogs and guide dogs for the blind. It is also used by the military, but at the same time is one of the most popular pet dogs of all time.

The Newfoundland: no other breed has such an affinity with water or has such an outstanding number of rescues to its credit. International Kennel Clubs generally describe the breed as having a sweet temperament, referring to it as the 'gentle giant.'

ALASKAN MALAMUTE

This large dog originating in Alaska is named after a local Inuit tribe. The Alaskan Malamute was bred for pulling sleds for long distances over the frozen terrain of Alaska and northern Canada. In fact, it is the largest of all the sled dogs. The breed was brought to the polar regions with the first peoples to settle the land. It was first shown outside its native lands in the 1920s.

Appearance A powerfully-built, handsome dog, the head is broad, with a skull that narrows toward the eyes. The muzzle is

large and the nose is usually black, although in red-and-white examples it is brown. The almond-shaped eyes are usually brown; darker shades are preferred, except in red-and-white dogs when they may be lighter. The ears are small and triangular and are normally held erect but may also be held close to the skull. The strong neck is carried on a deep-chested and powerfully built body with strong loins. The legs are well-muscled and strong. The tail may hang down at rest but is usually carried curled loosely over the back when working.

Coat Thick, coarse, outercoat; dense, oily and woolly undercoat. Colors range from solid white, gray, through to black, and from gold through red shades to liver; the underbody, legs, feet and mask are always white.

Size *Height:* male 25–28in (63.5–71cm); female 23–26in (58.5–66cm). *Weight:* 85–125lb (38.5–56.5kg).

Characteristics and Temperament
Although this strong dog is not especially fast, it needs plenty of exercise. It has the power to pull enormous weights for long distances – therefore it can also take some stopping if it has a mind not to stop. Quite a friendly animal, although not necessarily

One of the oldest of the Arctic sled dogs, the Alaskan Malamute was named after the Inuit tribe of Mahlemuts, which settled the shores of Kotzebue Sound, an arm of the Chukchi Sea in the western part of the state of Alaska. The origin of these people and their dogs is still unknown, but they were there for generations prior to the time when Asiatic sailors visited their shores, returning home with tales of people that used dogs to haul their sleds.

with other dogs, the Alaskan Malamute must receive careful training from an early age to ensure it is always under control. The dog makes an excellent guardian.

ANATOLIAN SHEPHERD DOG

This is a large herding and guard dog much prized by Anatolian shepherds in their native Turkey. Over many centuries, the breed was developed from mastiffs that had long existed in the Middle East and the Babylonian Empire. The dog is also known as the Karabash – a reference to its most familiar markings of cream and fawn, with a black mask and ears.

Appearance A tall, powerfully-built dog of the mastiff type. The head has a large, broad skull and a strong muzzle, square in outline. The nose is black. The rather small eyes are golden or brown and are set well apart. The triangular ears are also rather small compared with the size of the head and are pendent. A powerful, moderate-length neck is carried on a long body with a deep chest and a level back. The legs are long and well-boned. The long tail is carried low and slightly curled when at rest, but is carried curled over the back when the dog is alert and on the move.

Coat Close-lying and flat; short and dense with a thick undercoat; the hair on the neck, shoulders and tail is slightly thicker. Coat is often cream and fawn, with a black mask and ears, but all color patterns and markings are equally acceptable.

Size *Height:* male 29–32in (73.5–81.5cm); female 28–31in (71–79cm). *Weight:* male 110–141lb (50–64kg); female 90.5–130lb (41–59kg).

Characteristics and Temperament
A large, active, alert and intelligent dog, the Anatolian Shepherd was bred to guard, and that is still what it does best. The breed is extremely hardy but needs a large amount of food to keep its great bulk satisfied. It likes exercise, but is more inclined to move at a leisurely pace.

Believed to be many thousands of years old, the breed was once the Turkish shepherd's frontline defense against predators, having been developed to withstand a nomadic existence in the harsh environment of central Anatolia. First seen in the US in the 1950s, the Anatolian Shepherd Dog is not regarded as a glamorous breed, but as a fiercely independent working dog.

AUSTRALIAN CATTLE DOG

A tough breed developed to control cattle on the long journeys to market, the Australian Cattle Dog is also known by other names, including the Blue Heeler and the Australian Heeler – 'Heeler' being a reference to the dog's habit of nipping the heels of cattle when maneuvering them. The breed was developed initially in crossings involving sheepdogs, the Dingo, the Kelpie, the Dalmatian and the Bulldog. The breed, which has been pure since the 1890s, is a fairly recent arrival in Britain and America.

Appearance A compact, tough and symmetrical-looking dog with a typical sheep-herder's head. The head is wedge-shaped with a broad skull and a medium-length muzzle. The nose is black. The brown eyes are alert and intelligent. The ears are broad at the base, pricked and pointed. The neck is very strong and muscular. The body has a deep, broad chest and is carried on strong legs. The tail resembles that of a fox.

The Australian Cattle Dog was originally bred to guide cattle over long distances to bring them to auction. As a result, they have developed incredible stamina and are able to work all day without stopping.

162

Coat Hard, straight, weather-resistant outercoat; undercoat is short and dense. Colors are blue, blue-mottled or blue-speckled with tan, blue or black markings; or red-speckled with red markings.

Size *Height:* male 18–20in (46–51cm); female 17–19in (43–48cm). *Weight:* 35–44lb (16–20kg).

Characteristics and Temperament
Watchful and intelligent, the Australian Cattle Dog loves to work, being tireless and capable of fast movement. Loyal and easy to train, the breed is wary of strangers.

BEARDED COLLIE

Developed in Scotland from local sheepdogs, with a possible influx of genes from the Polish Lowland Sheepdog and the Komondor, the 'Beardie' is a sturdy member of the pastoral group. Today, it is one of the most popular and instantly recognizable of all the breeds, with a strong following both within the farming community and with those who simply appreciate its rascally good looks.

Appearance A long-coated, lean and active dog. The head has a broad, flat skull and a fairly long muzzle. The nose is usually black, but may be of a color harmonizing with the coat. The eyes also harmonize with the coat-color, and should be large, expressive and friendly. The ears are

moderately large and pendulous. The slightly arched neck is carried on a deep-chested body with strong loins. The legs are well-boned and muscular. The long tail is normally carried low, with a slight upward curl at the end, but extends when the dog is on the move.

Coat The outercoat is flat, strong and shaggy; the undercoat is soft and close; the coat should be long enough to enhance the shape of the dog and to form the characteristic beard. Colors are slate-gray, reddish-fawn, black, all shades of gray, brown and sand, with or without white markings.

Size *Height:* male 21–22in (53.5–56cm); female 20–21in (51–53.5cm). *Weight:* 39.5–59.5lb (18–27kg).

Characteristics and Temperament
An active, self-confident and fun-loving dog with an endearing expression, the Bearded Collie is many people's idea of the perfect pet – although it also makes a highly capable working dog. It is blessed with plenty of stamina and enjoys nothing more than a romp in the open air. The long hair is likely to pick up plenty of the countryside, however, so a thorough grooming is needed to keep the coat in first-class condition.

The Bearded Collie is one of Britain's oldest breeds, and while some believe it was around to greet the Romans when they invaded Britain, the current theory is that, like most shaggy-haired herding dogs, the Bearded Collie is descended from the Magyar Komondor of Central Europe.

BELGIAN SHEPHERD DOG

The Belgian Shepherd Dog has a history stretching back to the Middle Ages, but in the 1890s the breed was sub-divided according to three separate coat-types and four coat-color patterns. The basic body shape of each of these types remains the same, however. Each of the four types of Belgian Shepherd is named after a region in Belgium. These are the Groenendael; the Tervueren; the Malinois and the Laekenois. All of these dogs are sheepdogs and guardians, but they are increasingly regarded as pet dogs, too.

Appearance A medium to large, well-balanced and square dog, carrying itself elegantly and proudly; some types are slightly reminiscent of the German Shepherd. The head is fairly long, the skull and muzzle being almost equal in length; the muzzle tapers toward the nose, which is black. The brown eyes are almond-shaped, of medium size, and have a direct, quizzical expression. The ears are triangular, stiff and erect. The neck is well-muscled and broad at the shoulders. The body is deep-chested and powerful; the rump slopes slightly. The legs are well-boned and muscular. The tail is long.

Coat *Groenendael:* Outercoat long, straight and abundant and fairly harsh; undercoat dense; hair particularly long around the neck forming a ruff; fringe of long hair on back of fore legs; hair also long on tail and hindquarters; hair longer on dogs than on bitches. Color is black, or black with small amounts of white on chest and parts of the feet.
Tervueren: Coat similar to that of the Groenendael in length and texture. Colors are red, fawn or gray, with black tipping,

The American Kennel Club recognizes only the Groenendael under the name 'Belgian Sheepdog,' but also recognizes the Tervueren and the Malinois as individual breeds. The Laekenois can be registered and should eventually become fully recognized by the AKC. The Australian and New Zealand authorities recognize all four as separate breeds, while the Canadians, South Africans and the British follow the FCI classification scheme, recognizing all four as varieties of the same breed.

this feature being especially apparent on the shoulders, back and ribs.
Malinois: Coat thick and close; undercoat woolly; hair especially short on head, ears and lower legs; short on rest of body but thicker on tail and around neck; fringing on parts of the legs. Colors are similar to that of the Tervueren.
Laekenois: Coat is hard and wiry but not actually curled; about 2.5in (6cm) in length. Color is reddish-fawn with black shading, especially on the muzzle and tail.

Size *Height:* male 24–26in (61–66cm); female 22–24in (56–61cm). *Weight:* 60.5–63lb (27.5–28.5kg).

Characteristics and Temperament
An intelligent and alert breed that is also graceful and dignified. Loyal and obedient, the Belgian Shepherd is protective of its owner and property. These dogs require plenty of exercise.

The disposition of noble dogs is to be gentle with people they know and the opposite with those they don't know... How, then, can the dog be anything other than a lover of learning, since it defines what's its own and what's alien.

Plato

BERGAMASCO

This shepherd dog hails from Italy, where it has been used for centuries to guard livestock in the Alps lying to the north; here, the Bergamasco's distinctive cord-like coat may have helped protect it from wolves and the vagaries of climate. The breed became more generally known following its success at dog shows in the late 1940s.

Appearance A heavily- and uniquely-coated dog of medium size. The head has a broad skull, which is slightly convex between the ears; the muzzle tapers slightly toward the nose. The eyes are large and oval; usually chestnut, they convey calmness while also being alert. The ears are triangular in shape and semi-pendulous. The neck is strong, carried on a body with a broad, straight back. The legs are well-muscled. The tail is carried high when on the move, but low and slightly curled at the tip at other times.

Coat The coat has three types of hair; these are abundant, and form mats or flocks, starting from the spine and going down the flanks to reach the ground. Coat-color can range from gray or silver-gray (merle) to black with brown shades also intermixed – colors that may have served as a camouflage when working in the mountains.

Size *Height:* 21–25in (53–63.5cm). *Weight:* male 70–84lb (32–38kg); female 56–70lb (25.5–32kg).

An ancient breed that can be traced back thousands of years to Persia (Iran), where hardy, vigorous shepherding dogs worked with nomadic tribes, tending their flocks in harsh mountain environments. Certain of these nomads ultimately settled in the Italian Alps and remained there, their dogs developing into the breed seen there today.

Characteristics and Temperament
A dog with highly protective instincts. Cautious by nature, the Bergamasco is also intelligent and vigilant. Born with short, smooth fur, the characteristic mats develop as the dog grows, but once fully-flocked the coat requires very little care, apart from the occasional brushing and bathing.

BERNESE MOUNTAIN DOG

It is likely that the foundations of this large, affable breed were laid when local Swiss herding dogs and a type of guard dog, brought by invading Romans into what is now Switzerland, were crossed about 2,000 years ago. A powerful animal, the Bernese Mountain Dog has long been used to pull small carts loaded with produce to market. The dog gets its name from the Swiss canton of Berne. A popular dog in Europe, it is less common elsewhere, although its friendly nature will always win admirers wherever it is seen.

Appearance A stocky, well-balanced dog with an attractive coat. The head has a broad skull and a medium-sized muzzle. The almond-shaped eyes are dark brown and convey a kindly expression. The ears are medium-sized and triangular. A strong and muscular neck is carried on a compact body with a deep chest and a strong, level back. The legs are strongly boned and well-muscled. The bushy tail is raised when on the move.

Coat Long, soft and silky; a slight wave is permitted, but the coat should not be curly. The color is jet black with russet-brown or tan markings; a white blaze is present on the head and a white cross on the chest; white paws and a white tail-tip are also desirable.

Size *Height:* male 25–27.5in (63.5–70cm); female 23–26in (58.5–66cm). *Weight:* 87–90lb (39.5–41kg).

Characteristics and Temperament
A delightful and well-mannered character, full of good humor and responsive to training. The Bernese Mountain Dog

makes the perfect companion for a country-dweller. It has an easy-going way and should be encouraged to exercise regularly to avoid becoming overweight.

The Bernese Mountain Dog is a striking. tricolored dog. Males appear instantly masculine, while bitches have a recognizably feminine appearance.

BORDER COLLIE

Recognized the world over as one of the finest and most intelligent of all sheepdogs, the Border Collie was formerly used in the border regions of England, Scotland and Wales, but is now found far and wide. The breed was well-established by the mid-19th century, and a comprehensive stud book and registration system has been in operation in Britain for many years. However, the breed was only registered by the UK Kennel Club in 1976, since when the dog has featured widely in the show ring as well as in obedience trials. This agile and clever dog has also been used to great effect in rescue work and for sniffing out illegal substances.

Appearance A graceful, balanced dog with a low-slung body. The head has a fairly

The Border Collie has the unique working style of gathering and fetching stock using wide, sweeping outruns, then controlling the sheep with an intense gaze, coupled with a stalking movement to bring them together. The dog also has extraordinary instinct and an uncanny ability to reason things out for itself when out of the shepherd's sight.

broad skull and a fairly short, straight muzzle tapering toward the nose. The nose is usually black but may be brown, chocolate or slate to harmonize with other coat-colors. The oval eyes are brown, but in merles (dilutions of the overall body-color) one or both may be blue. The ears are medium-sized and carried semi-erect or erect. The strong, slightly-arched neck sits on a long, athletic-looking body with a deep chest. The medium-length legs are strong and muscular. The tail is moderately long and raised when on the move but never carried over the back.

Coat Moderately long; the outercoat is dense and medium-textured, and the undercoat is soft and dense. Various colors are possible, including black, black-and-white, and tan-and-white.

Size *Height:* male 21in (53.5cm); female 20in (51cm). *Weight:* male 52lb (23.5kg); female 42lb (19kg).

Characteristics and Temperament
Keen, alert, responsive, hard-working and intelligent: these are some of the qualities that have made the Border Collie such a successful farm dog. The breed is also loyal and faithful and responds well to commands. However, these attributes mean that pet dogs of this breed can become destructive and difficult if they do not receive adequate exercise for both body and mind.

BOUVIER DES FLANDRES

The Bouvier des Flandres was originally bred for herding and protecting cattle in Belgium, also France. In fact, the name translates as 'Flanders Ox-driver.' After the First World War, during which the dog was also used as an ambulance dog and messenger, the breed was rescued from near-extinction by a Belgian army vet who saved one dog. Today, this big, amiable breed has also found favor as a house pet as well as being used for police work.

Appearance A strongly-built and powerful dog with a large head and a compact body. The head has a flat, wide skull and a broad, powerful muzzle. The nose is black. The oval eyes should be as dark as possible and convey intelligence. The ears are triangular. The neck is strong and thickens toward the shoulders. The body is short, deep and strong. The legs are strong, well-muscled and of medium length. The tail is usually docked.

Coat A coarse, rugged and thick coat about 2.5in (6cm) in length; the undercoat is dense; the hair around the mouth should form a thick beard, and with the prominent eyebrows give the dog a somewhat fearsome expression. Colors range from fawn to black, including brindle; there may be a white star on the chest.

Size *Height:* male 25–27in (63.5–68.5cm); female 23–25.5in (58.5–65cm). *Weight:* *Recognized by the AKC in 1929, the Bouvier was admitted to the stud book in 1931. It was imported regularly from Europe until the Second World War, following which interest revived and the American Bouvier des Flandres Club was established in 1963.*

male 77–88lb (35–40kg); female 59–77lb (27–35kg).

Characteristics and Temperament
Although this large dog has a faintly forbidding appearance, it is in fact good-natured, calm and trustworthy, and makes an alert and effective guard dog. Only moderate exercise is required, and the Bouvier is likely to settle easily into family life.

BOXER

The likely ancestors of the Boxer are the Bulldog and the Great Dane. A German breed, the Boxer has existed in the form seen today for over 100 years. The breed became unpopular during the First World War, but its popularity was later restored – no doubt due mainly to its virtues as a guard dog and active companion. In America and Germany, Boxers have cropped ears, but in Britain they are left uncropped.

Appearance Clean and hard in appearance, the Boxer is a squarely-built and active dog. The head is short and square, its skin forming wrinkles. The muzzle is broad and deep, with the lower jaw undershot and curving slightly upward. The nose is black. The dark-brown eyes face well forward and impart a lively and alert expression. The ears are set widely apart at the top of the skull and lie flat to the cheeks when resting, falling forward when alert; ears may be cropped and erect in some countries. The neck is round and strong. The body is short and deep-chested with a strong, slightly sloping, straight back. The muscular legs are moderately long and terminate in cat-like feet. The tail is usually docked.

Coat Short, hard and glossy. Colors are shades of fawn or brindle, with white.

Size *Height:* male 22.5–25in (57–63.5cm); female 21–23in (53.5–58.5cm). *Weight:* male 66–70lb (30–32kg); female 55–60lb (25–27kg).

Characteristics and Temperament
An extrovert by nature, the Boxer is fearless and confident. Although loyal to family and friends, it can be wary of strangers and therefore makes an efficient guard dog. The Boxer needs firm handling to remind it who is in charge – especially when in the presence of other dogs with whom it tends to become rather unfriendly.

The Boxer needs firm handling and an energetic owner. Not only will it guard your children with its life, but it will also fiercely protect your property.

BRIARD

There is a legend from the 14th century that a type of dog similar in appearance to the modern Briard saved the life of the son of Aubry de Montdidier, leading to it becoming known as the 'Chien d'Aubry.' A rather more likely explanation may be that the breed hails from Brie, in France, where undoubtedly it was used for herding sheep and as a guardian. It has also found employment as a pack dog for the army, but nowadays is mostly kept as a rumbustious but friendly pet.

Appearance Muscular and well-proportioned with a long, flowing coat.

The head has a slightly rounded skull and a square, strong muzzle. The nose is black. The large, dark-brown eyes have a gentle and intelligent expression. The ears are fairly short and must not hang too close to the head. The neck is moderately long and arched. The deep-chested body has a firm and level back and is carried on strongly-boned, well-muscled legs. The tail is fairly long with an upward curl at the tip.

Coat Long and slightly wavy with a dense undercoat; the head sports a beard, mustache, and eyebrows that form a veil over the eyes. Colors are black, slate-gray or various shades of fawn.

History credits both the Marquis de Lafayette and Thomas Jefferson with introducing specimens of the Briard to the Americas.

Size *Height:* male 24–27in (61–68.5cm); female 23–25.5in (58.5–65cm). *Weight:* male 85lb (38.5kg); female 75lb (34kg).

Characteristics and Temperament
The Briard has an effortless gait, seemingly gliding over the ground. A friendly and extrovert dog, and good with children, the Briard can on occasions get a little over-boisterous during play. This is a dog that likes plenty of exercise.

BULLMASTIFF

The Bullmastiff came about through crossings between the Bulldog and the Old English Mastiff. The dog was used as a very effective guard dog and gamekeeper's dog – in fact, it was often known as 'the gamekeeper's dog.' A strong animal, but highly amenable to training and correct handling, the Bullmastiff was officially recognized as a breed in 1924, although it had been in existence well before that date.

Appearance A powerful and symmetrical dog with a smooth coat. The head has a square skull and a deep, strong muzzle. The skin on the head becomes wrinkled when the dog is aroused. The eyes are hazel or darker in color and of medium size. Ears are V-shaped and folded, helping to accentuate the impression of squareness to the skull. The neck is very muscular and almost as wide as the skull. The body is short with a broad chest and a straight back and is carried on powerful legs of moderate length. The tail is long and tapering.

Coat Short and hard and lying flat to the body. Colors may be any shade of brindle, fawn or red.

Size *Height:* male 25–27in (63.5–68.5cm); female 24–26in (61–66cm). *Weight:* male

The Bullmastiff is a large and powerful breed, unsuitable for the novice dog-handler. It was recognized by the AKC in 1933.

110–130lb (50–59kg); female 90–110lb (41–50kg).

Characteristics and Temperament
A powerful and purposeful dog with an independent streak, the Bullmastiff is not recommended for the novice dog-owner. It is reliable, faithful and affectionate, however, and makes an excellent guard dog. The Bullmastiff can also cover the ground with remarkable speed and agility for a dog of such commanding size and build.

ROUGH COLLIE

The Rough Collie probably evolved from dogs brought to Britain by the Romans in the period after 50 BC, which bred with native dogs and is, apart from coat-length, the same as the Smooth Collie. The Rough Collie achieved royal recognition when Queen Victoria kept the breed at Balmoral Castle in Scotland. Today, although the Rough Collie is more likely to be seen in the show ring than working on the hills with sheep, it nevertheless retains many of its herding instincts. The breed found immortal fame in the *Lassie* books and movies.

Appearance An attractively-coated, well-proportioned dog. The wedge-shaped head has a flat and fairly wide skull and a long muzzle. The nose is black. The eyes are medium-sized and almond-shaped and should impart a gentle expression; the color is dark brown, except in blue merle-coated dogs, when they are blue or blue-flecked.

The ears are held back when at rest, but when the dog is alert they are brought forward and held semi-erect. The neck is powerful and arched, and is carried on a rather long body with a deep chest. The legs are strongly boned and terminate in oval feet. The long tail is held low at rest,

raised when the dog is on the move, but never over the back.

Coat Very dense, the outercoat being straight and harsh; undercoat soft and close; mane and frill very abundant. Colors are sable-and-white, tricolor, or blue merle; all colors also include white.

Size *Height:* male 22–24in (56–61cm); female 20–22in (51–56cm). *Weight:* male 45–65lb (20.5–29.5kg); female 40–55lb (18–25kg).

Characteristics and Temperament This elegant and beautiful dog makes the ideal pet, being friendly and loyal, especially toward its owner. The luxuriant coat needs plenty of grooming to retain its optimum condition.

The show version of the Rough Collie has been developed over more than 100 years and is quite distant from its working ancestor; it is possible that Borzoi was introduced at some stage, which would account for the narrow head-shape with minimal stop, and the slight rise over the loins.

SMOOTH COLLIE

This breed is essentially a short-coated version of the Rough Collie, and its ancestry is the same. Many consider the Smooth Collie to be the more attractive and practical of the two.

Appearance A dog of dignified appearance, giving the impression of ability in the field. The wedge-shaped head has a flat and fairly wide skull and a long muzzle. The nose is black. The eyes are medium-sized and almond-shaped and should convey gentleness; the color is dark brown except in blue merle-coated dogs when they are blue or blue-flecked. The ears are held back when resting, but when the dog is alert they are brought forward and held semi-erect. The neck is powerful and arched, and is carried on a rather long body with a deep

chest. The legs are strongly boned terminating in oval feet. The long tail is held low at rest but raised when on the move, although never over the back.

Coat The outercoat is short, flat and harsh; the undercoat is dense. Colors are sable-and-white, tricolor, or blue merle; all colors may also include white.

Size *Height:* male 22–24in (56–61cm); female 20–22in (51–56cm). *Weight:* 40–65lb (18–29.5kg).

Characteristics and Temperament
This elegant dog makes an ideal pet, being friendly and loyal, especially toward its owner. More of a working dog than its close relative, the Rough Collie, this breed expects correspondingly more exercise.

Smooth Collies should not be left alone for long periods, as they are easily bored, being prone to barking if not taught good manners.

DOBERMANN

The breed takes its name from Herr Louis Dobermann, a German tax collector who bred the dog in the 1870s. He crossed a variety of dogs, including German Shepherd, Pinscher, Rottweiler and Manchester Terrier to produce an animal capable of protecting him – and also of encouraging recalcitrant debtors to pay up! Given its pedigree, it is not surprising that the Dobermann reflects many virtues, including speed, strength and intelligence. In America, where the breed is extremely popular, it is usually referred to as the Dobermann Pinscher.

Appearance Muscular and elegant with a smooth, glossy coat, the head has a fairly narrow, flat skull with a rather long, deep muzzle. The nose is solid black in black dogs, dark brown in brown dogs, dark gray in blue individuals and light brown in fawn dogs. The eyes are fairly deep-set and should convey a lively and intelligent expression. The neat ears may be erect or dropped; in some countries they are docked. A long and lean neck is carried on a deep-chested body with a short, firm back. The legs are long and well-boned and terminate in cat-like feet. The tail is usually docked.

Coat Smooth, short and close-lying. Colors are black, blue, brown or fawn, with tan markings above the eyes, on the muzzle, throat, chest, legs, feet and tail.

Size *Height:* male 27in (68.5cm); female 25.5in (65cm). *Weight:* male 83lb (37.5kg); female 73lb (33kg).

Characteristics and Temperament
Unfortunately, the Dobermann has suffered an image problem in the past, having been seen primarily as a rather fierce guard dog. However, the breed can make a highly intelligent, loyal and delightful pet for owners willing to train it carefully from puppyhood, and to be firm and consistent in handling the dog, so that it knows who is in charge. Careful selection has largely reduced the propensity for wayward and ill-tempered behavior often seen previously. The dog requires plenty of exercise but is easy to groom.

During the Second World War, US Marines used Dobermanns to flush out enemy forces, earning them the nickname, Devil Dogs, with the result that many are still intimidated by the breed today. Twenty-five such war dogs died during the Battle of Guam in 1944.

ESKIMO DOG

The American Eskimo Dog is a breed of companion and semi-sled dog originating in the USA. It has also been used as a watchdog, and achieved popularity in the 1930s and '40s as a circus performer – even walking the tightrope! The Eskie is derived almost completely from the various German Spitz breeds, crossed with Japanese Spitz and Keeshonden. The Nordic Spitz family is one of the least altered by human intervention and reflects most closely the prototypical dog from which the Eskimo was derived.

Appearance The standard for the American Eskimo Dog is that it be white or white and biscuit-cream, with the distinctive black points (lips, nose, and eye-rims). Eyes are brown (blue eyes are undesirable). The body is compact, its length being only slightly greater than its height at the shoulder. The muzzle is long and wolf-like. The ears are held erect and alert, and the tail is richly plumed and held loosely curled on the back.

Coat The white double coat consists of a short, dense undercoat, with longer guard hairs growing through to form the outercoat, which is straight with no curl or wave. The coat is thicker and longer around the neck and chest, forming a ruff, which is more pronounced in dogs than in bitches. The rump and hind legs, down to the hocks, are also covered in thicker, longer hair to form the characteristic britches.

Size These dogs closely resemble smaller versions of the Samoyed, and come in three standard sizes: the Toy, that is from 9–13in (23–33cm) at the withers; the Miniature, from 12–15in (31–38cm); the Standard, from 16 inches up to and including 21 inches (41–53cm).

The Eskie was recognized by the AKC in 1994, setting the current standard for the breed. Already accepted by the United Kennel Club, there is no difference between the two breed standards except that the AKC recognizes the Toy size and the UKC does not.

Characteristics and Temperament
Because the breed is so attractive, many purchase puppies without doing sufficient research. These are very intelligent dogs and need to be stimulated to avoid behavioral problems; this can be achieved by early obedience training or participation in dog sports. On the other hand, Eskies were intended to be companion dogs, and thrive on being a part of a human family.

ESTRELA MOUNTAIN DOG

The huge Estrela Mountain Dog comes from the Serra da Estrela region of central Portugal where it has long been used for guarding and herding livestock. It is not known whether the ancestors that contributed to the breed were brought by the Romans, when they colonized the Iberian Peninsula, or arrived later with invading Visigoths, but it is undoubtedly an ancient breed. Relatively rare outside its native land, the Estrela's equable temperament should see it winning over plenty of converts in the future. The breed exists in long-coated and short-coated forms.

Appearance A sturdy, mastiff-type dog. The head is long and strong with a broad, slightly-domed skull. The muzzle is slightly tapering, and the nose is black. The eyes are medium-sized and oval and amber in color. The ears are smallish, triangular and carried at the sides of the head. The neck is short and thick and is carried on a body with a broad, muscular back, a deep chest and slightly-arched loins. The legs are well-boned and muscular. The tail is long and well-furred.

Coat *Long-coated:* Outercoat thick, close-lying and fairly harsh; it may be flat or slightly wavy; the undercoat is dense. *Short-coated:* Thick, short, fairly harsh and

The Estrela Mountain Dog will fiercely protect its pack (family), come what may.

straight with a short, dense undercoat. Colors are fawn, brindle, or wolf-gray.

Size *Height:* male 25.5–28.5in (65–72.5cm); female 24.5–27in (62–68.5cm). *Weight:* 66–110lb (30–50kg).

Characteristics and Temperament
This large dog is remarkably well-disposed toward its friends and family, although it can be stubborn on occasions. Easy to groom and undemanding in its feeding habits, it makes a good companion and guard dog for an active family.

GERMAN SHEPHERD DOG

One of the most popular and instantly recognizable dogs anywhere, the German Shepherd is a byword for excellence and versatility throughout the canine world. Bred to the standard we know today in the later part of the 19th century by German army officer, Max von Stephanitz, the breed was originally used as a sheep-herder. Later, however, it found favor as a police and military dog, and during the First World War nearly 50,000 were used by the German army. By 1926 it was the most popular dog in Britain, where it was often called the Alsatian Wolf Dog, the term 'Alsatian' being still in use to

With correct training, the German Shepherd can be taught to do just about any job, and do it well.

Coat The outercoat is close, straight, hard and weather-resistant; the undercoat is thick, woolly and close. Colors include black, black-and-tan, and sable; occasionally white or cream dogs appear, also long-coated varieties, which are not generally accepted for show purposes.

Size *Height:* male 25in (63.5cm); female 23in (58.5cm). *Weight:* male 80.5lb (36.5kg); female 65lb (29.5kg).

Characteristics and Temperament
A good-quality German Shepherd Dog makes a highly trainable, tireless, intelligent and loyal companion. The dog is also excellent in a variety of working roles. It has supple movements, with a long-reaching gait. The dog needs plenty of exercise to keep body and mind occupied, although some have a tendency to be lazy if given the chance.

describe the breed. Poor breeding and thoughtless handling – coupled with the dog's widespread use as a guard dog – unfortunately resulted in it gaining a reputation for aggressive and unpredictable behavior. However, the best examples of the breed are dogs which cannot be praised too highly. Today, the German Shepherd excels in its various roles, including police and military work, tracking, leading the blind, guarding, drug detection and, of course, being a perfect companion for someone prepared to offer the kind of life this intelligent dog deserves.

Appearance An alert, long-bodied, purposeful-looking dog. The head has a moderately-broad skull and a long muzzle. The eyes are almond-shaped, usually brown, and should convey intelligence and confidence. The ears are medium-sized, broad at the base, and carried erect. The neck is long, strong and muscular. The deep-chested body is long with a straight back that slopes toward the hindquarters; the body-length should be slightly greater than the dog's height. The legs are strong and muscular. The tail is long and bushy and hangs in a curve when standing.

GIANT SCHNAUZER

This is the largest of the three Schnauzer breeds, used in Bavaria in Germany as long ago as the 15th century for herding duties. It started to become redundant in this role when railways became a more economical option for moving cattle from place to place. However, the Giant Schnauzer's impressive size and appearance meant that it soon found favor in the cities of Germany as a guard dog; for a time, it was known as the Munich Schnauzer. The breed is now popular both as a guardian companion dog and as a police dog.

Appearance A powerful, long-legged and almost square dog. The head has a fairly broad skull and a long, strong muzzle. The nose is black. The eyes are oval and dark. The V-shaped ears drop forward to the temple. The strong neck is slightly arched and is carried on a body with a broad, deep chest and a strong, straight back. The legs are long and well-boned. The tail is customarily docked.

Coat The outercoat is hard and wiry, and there should be a good undercoat; beard, mustache and eyebrows are a prominent feature. Colors are pure black or pepper-and-salt.

The Giant Schnauzer is pictured below with its Miniature cousin (see also page 144), the third type being the Standard Schnauzer (see page 148).

Size *Height:* male 25.5–27.5in (65–70cm); female 23.5–25.5in (60–65cm). *Weight:* male 100lb (45.5kg); female 90lb (41kg).

Characteristics and Temperament
Intelligent, strong and active, the Giant Schnauzer is also friendly and reliable. However, its size and boldness mean that it can also make a very effective deterrent to a would-be burglar. The coat needs stripping twice-yearly to keep it in good order.

GREAT DANE

Despite its name, the Great Dane is of German origin and not Danish, and it has been the national dog of Germany since 1876. More recently, it was named the state dog of Pennsylvania, USA, in 1965.

Originally used to hunt wild boar, the breed was initially classed as a hound, and it undoubtedly has hound blood – possibly Irish Wolfhound, and perhaps English Mastiff – in its makeup. Another misconception is that it is aggressive, when in fact it is the archetypal gentle giant.

Appearance Muscular, elegant and of imposing appearance, the head has a flattish skull and a deep, broad muzzle. The eyes are round, medium-sized and dark in color; in harlequins odd, or wall eyes are permissible. The ears are triangular and folded forward; in some

countries, such as America, the ears are docked. The neck is long, arched and held high. The body is deep, with slightly-arched loins. The legs are long and muscular and terminate in cat-like feet. The long tail tapers to the tip.

Coat Short, dense and glossy. Colors are brindles, fawns, blues, black, or harlequins (pure white background with black or blue patches that appear torn or ragged).

Size *Height:* male 30in (76cm); female 28in (71cm) – these are minimum height requirements. *Weight:* male 119lb (54kg); female 101.5lb (46kg).

Great Danes are among the tallest breeds, along with the Irish Wolfhound. In August 2004, a Great Dane from Grass Valley, California, was recognized by the Guinness Book of Records as the world's tallest dog. It measured 42.2in (107cm) at the withers.

Characteristics and Temperament
Spirited, courageous, always friendly and dependable, and never timid or aggressive, the Great Dane is a majestic-looking dog with a dignified air. It is really only suitable for those with space to house this huge dog and the budget to keep up with its great appetite. Devoted to its family, the Great Dane is an endearing character but sadly has a relatively short lifespan.

HOVAWART

This is a breed originating from the Black Forest region of Bavaria in Germany, where it was first described in books and paintings in medieval times. The name Hovawart means 'farmyard warden,' and dogs of this type were known to guard farms as far back as the 1200s. Only seen in Britain since about the mid 1970s and in America since the 1980s, the breed was first recognized by the German Kennel Club in 1936.

Appearance A medium-sized dog with a strong physique. The head is fairly long with a broad skull and a gently-tapering muzzle. The nose-color should match the

Hovawarts, being fundamentally working dogs, require consistent, loving, yet strict training, together with very regular activity throughout their lives.

coat. The eyes are oval and have an alert expression; they should be as dark as possible. The ears are triangular and pendent. The neck is of medium length and carried on a moderately long body. The legs are strong and muscular. The tail is long and bushy and carried high when the dog is on the move.

Coat Medium-length but shorter on the face and front legs; the undercoat is fine and light. Colors are black-and-gold, blond, or black.

Size *Height:* male 24–27.5in (61–70cm); female 23–25.5in (58.5–65cm). *Weight:* male 66–88lb (30–40kg); female 55–77lb (25–35kg).

Characteristics and Temperament
A playful dog and quite devoted to its family, the Hovawart can nevertheless become domineering when other dogs are involved. Easy to feed and groom, it is a good choice as a companion, but can be somewhat reserved as far as strangers are concerned.

When the Man waked up he said,
'What is Wild Dog doing here?'
And the Woman said,
'His name is not Wild Dog any more,
but the First Friend,
because he will be our friend
for always and always and always.'

Rudyard Kipling

HUNGARIAN KUVASZ

Some claim the Kuvasz had connections with the Hun, a nomadic Asiatic tribe, while others describe it as the sheepdog that accompanied Turkish refugees and their flocks fleeing the Mongols to arrive in Hungary in 1200. The Kuvasz came into its own in the 15th century at the court of Matyas I, who claimed to trust only his Kuvasz dogs and not his people; the dogs reverted to being sheepdogs after the king died. The breed may have contributed to the development of several similar sheepdogs, such as the Polish Tatra, the Italian Maremma, the Pyrenean, and the Anatolian Shepherd.

Appearance Large, sturdy and powerful, the head has a long, slightly-arched skull and a broad, slightly-tapering muzzle. Eyes are almond-shaped, dark-brown and set widely apart. Ears are V-shaped and folded. The neck is long and muscular, carried on a fairly long, deep body. The legs are powerful, the hind feet longer than the fore. The tail is carried level when on the move, with a slight upward curve to the tip.

Coat The outercoat is slightly wavy, and medium to coarse; the undercoat is woolly and fine. Coat-color is white to cream.

Size *Height:* male 28–29in (71–73.5cm); female 26–27.5in (66–70cm). *Weight:* male

Kuvasz (plural Kuvaszok) most likely comes from the Turkic word kavas, *meaning guard or soldier, or* kuwasz, *meaning protector.*

88–114lb (40–52kg); female 66–92lb (30–43kg).

Characteristics and Temperament
An attractive dog, but by no means one of the easiest to keep as a pet. Although the Kuvasz is gentle and loyal with those it knows, it is a dog that was bred to guard, and still considers guarding an important part of its life. It is therefore wary of strangers and likes to have somewhere it can patrol. Big and burly, it also has a large appetite.

KELPIE

This Australian breed came about in the latter half of the 19th century, when imported English Collies were mated with local breeds. The Kelpie was first shown in 1908, since when it has proved its worth, mustering and droving, with little or no guidance or command, on the vast sheep stations of Australia.

Appearance A tough and muscular little sheepdog with a fox-like face. The head has a flat skull and a slightly-tapering muzzle. The brown eyes convey a lively and intelligent expression. The ears are large, wide at the base, and held erect. The powerful neck is carried on a body slightly longer than the dog's height; the chest is broad. The strong legs are of medium length, ending in cat-like feet. The bushy tail is usually carried low.

Coat Short and smooth, with a harsh, glossy outercoat. Colors are black, black-

and-tan, red, red-and-tan, fawn, smoke-blue or chocolate.

Size *Height:* male 18–20in (46–51cm); female 17–19in (43–48cm). *Weight:* 25–45lb (11.5–20.5kg).

Characteristics and Temperament
The Kelpie is a tireless worker in its native land, where its tough constitution, weatherproof coat, and keen intelligence makes it a highly-regarded sheepdog.

Working Kelpies are bred for their natural working ability and aren't usually selected by reason of their appearance. Breeders tend to call their breeding establishments 'studs,' in the manner of other types of stud farm.

KOMONDOR

Another of the cord-coated breeds, this dog resembles the Hungarian Puli, although it is somewhat larger. The Hungarian Komondor's coat helps it to blend in with the flocks of sheep that it guards. Its origin is debatable: some say it was a dog of the Magyars, while others believe it to be Sumerian in origin. The most likely explanation is that the dogs were brought by the Cumans, a nomadic Turkic people who inhabited a vague area north of the Black Sea, and who settled in Hungary during the 12th and 13th centuries. In recent times, an explosion in the coyote population in the United States, and a reluctance to use poison, has led to the renaissance of the Komondor as a sheepdog.

Appearance A big, muscular dog, the head has a broad, arched skull and a broad, deep muzzle. The nose is black. The eyes should be as dark as possible and not too deeply set. The ears are medium-sized, U-shaped and pendent. The strong neck is carried on a body with a deep, muscular chest. The legs are strongly boned and muscular. The tail is slightly curved at the tip and is raised to the horizontal position when the dog is excited.

Coat A long, coarse outercoat and a soft undercoat; the hair forms tassels giving a corded appearance; it may take two years

The Komondor's unique dreadlock appearance gives a hint of a common origin with the Puli and the Bergamasco, and there may also be a link between the Komondor and the South Russian Ovcharka.

for the coat to grow to its full length. Coat-color is always white.

Size *Height:* 26–32in (66–81cm). *Weight:* 80–135lb (36–61kg).

Characteristics and Temperament
Despite its unusual and disreputable-looking coat, the Komondor makes a devoted companion, but constant care of the coat is demanding. Bred for the countryside, it is not suited to life in town.

MAREMMA

The Maremma Sheepdog is used to guard flocks and property in its native Italy. The breed's exact origins are unknown, but it is possible that it is a descendant of the dogs owned by the wandering Magyar peoples. The temperament of examples seen outside of Italy is reported to have improved considerably over the years.

Appearance A large, muscular dog with a thick white coat. The skull is wide between the ears but narrows toward the eyes; the muzzle is fairly long and tapers slightly

toward the nose – the whole head being slightly conical in shape. The nose is black. The eyes are almond-shaped and dark brown in color. The V-shaped ears hang flat by the side of the head but move forward when the dog is alert. A strong neck is carried on a fairly long, broad body with a deep chest. The medium-length, large-boned legs end in large, almost round feet. The long tail is carried almost level with the back when on the move.

Coat Thick, long and harsh with a thick undercoat; the coat is sometimes slightly wavy. The color is all-white, but slight fawn or ivory shades may be present.

Size *Height:* male 25.5–28.5in (65–72.5cm); female 23.5–26.5in (60–67.5cm). *Weight:* male 66–99lb (30–45kg).

Characteristics and Temperament
Despite its size, the Maremma is capable of moving easily over rough terrain and of turning quickly. Intelligent and brave, although not aggressive, the breed is rather aloof and naturally wary of strangers but makes a good guarding companion when properly trained.

The Maremma Sheepdog may be related to other large, white European guardian dogs, including the Pyrenean, the Hungarian Kuvasz, and the Turkish Akbash.

MASTIFF

This huge breed is one of the oldest in Britain, and dogs similar in appearance to the modern breed were to be found in Britain at the time of the Romans, fighting alongside their masters as they tried to repel the invaders. Later, recognizing the breed's great strength, courage and presence, the Romans took Mastiffs back to Rome to take part in gladiatorial contests against animals such as bulls, lions and bears. The dog's popularity went into a decline in Britain after the Second World War but was revived using imported stock. The Mastiff is also known as the Old English Mastiff.

Appearance A massive, powerfully-built dog with a large, heavily-jowled head. The head has a square skull, a short, broad muzzle, and a marked stop. The small eyes are set widely apart, are brown in color, and convey calm and strength. The ears are small and thin and hang down by the sides of the head. The neck is highly muscular. The body has a deep, wide chest and a very muscular back and loins. The legs are large-boned and muscular. The tail tapers at the tip and is held slightly curved when on the move.

Coat The coat is short. Colors are apricot-fawn, silver-fawn, fawn or fawn brindle.

Size *Height:* 27.5–30in (70–76cm). *Weight:* 174–190lb (79–86g).

Characteristics and Temperament
Fortunately, this large and impressive dog is docile and good-natured, but it still makes an admirable guard dog. It is affectionate and loyal and needs plenty of human company and reasonable amounts of exercise. The Mastiff also has a prodigious appetite – as befits a dog of its size – and this should be taken into account when ownership is being considered.

In terms of body mass, the Mastiff is the largest of the dogs, but the Irish Wolfhound and the Great Dane are the tallest.

NEAPOLITAN MASTIFF

The Neapolitan Mastiff is another very old breed, thought to be a descendant of the Molossus breed of ancient Roman times. Because of its huge strength and size, the dog was once used for fighting, although it also found favor as a guard dog and for pulling carts. It is also reported to have been used for fighting against lions in the Colosseum and other ancient Roman arenas. The painter Piero Scanziani established a kennel for the breed and is credited with its revival and promotion; the dog was first shown in 1946. In its native Italy, the Neapolitan Mastiff is sometimes seen with cropped ears.

Appearance A muscular, powerfully-built dog with a massive head. The head has a wide skull and a short, square and deep muzzle. The fairly large, chestnut-brown or black eyes have a penetrating expression. The ears are short with triangular tips and usually hang down, although in some countries they are cropped. The neck is short and massive. The body has a broad, muscular chest and is fairly short and deep. The legs are powerful and well-boned. The tail tapers toward the tip; it may be docked by one third of its length

Coat Short, dense and fine, with a glossy sheen. Color is preferably black, but blue, gray and brown are permitted.

Obedience is important in the Neapolitan, in that it is generally tolerant of pain due to its early fighting background and the fact that its skin is loose on the body.

Size *Height:* 26–29in (66–73.5cm). *Weight:* 110–154lb (50–70kg).

Characteristics and Temperament
The dog's gait can be described as bear-like, and it rarely runs at a gallop. Reliable, obedient and not aggressive unless provoked or commanded to attack, the breed is nevertheless not one for the inexperienced owner. Its loose jowls and pendulous lips mean that it is somewhat inclined to slobber and dribble.

NEWFOUNDLAND

The exact origins of the Newfoundland are somewhat obscure, but it is possible that the breed developed from a type of dog that was brought by nomadic peoples into the northern polar regions and not actually from Newfoundland itself. From there, the breed was taken by sailors and traders to England, where it became very popular.

Appearance A big-boned, strong-looking dog. The head is broad and massive with a short, square muzzle. The dark-brown eyes are small and deep-set. The ears are also small and fall close to the sides of the head. A strong neck is carried on a deep-chested body with muscular loins. The legs are of moderate length and strongly boned, terminating in webbed feet – an invaluable aid to swimming. The tail is of medium length.

Coat An oily, waterproof, double coat; the coat is flat and dense. Colors are black, brown (chocolate or bronze), or landseer – this last color, named for Sir Edwin Landseer, who painted the breed on many occasions, being white with black markings.

The Newfoundland must be a large dog to perform the duties for which it has become justly famous, with the strength and ability to bring ashore a drowning man, and to swim great distances through icy waters.

Size *Height:* male 28in (71cm); female 26in (66cm). *Weight:* male 140–150lb (63.5–68kg); female 110–120lb (50–54.5kg).

Characteristics and Temperament
When one thinks of dogs and water, the name Newfoundland invariably springs to mind, for no other breed has such a natural

affinity with the element. Used for centuries to help fishermen retrieve their nets, the Newfoundland also has a deserved reputation as a powerful swimmer and life-saver. On land, the nautical theme is continued, for the dog moves along with a

Beauty without vanity, strength without insolence, courage without ferocity, and all the virtues of man without his vices...

Lord Byron (of his Newfoundland)

slightly rolling gait. Resembling a cuddly bear, especially in puppyhood, the Newfoundland grows into a delightful character – affectionate, docile and willing to please – but also capable of guarding family and home.

NORWEGIAN BUHUND

A Spitz-type breed, the Norwegian Buhund is a herding and guard dog. The word Buhund means 'the dog found on the homestead.' It is closely related to the Icelandic Sheepdog and the Jämthund. The Buhund was only recognized officially in the early part of the 20th century.

Appearance A lightly-built, compact dog. The head is wedge-shaped, with a flat skull and a tapering muzzle. The nose is black. The eyes are dark brown, conveying alertness and fearlessness. The tall ears are held erect and are very mobile. A medium-length neck is carried on a short, strong body with a deep chest. The medium-length legs are lean and strong. The tail is short and thick and carried curled over the back in typical Spitz fashion.

Coat The outercoat is hard and smooth; the undercoat is soft and woolly. Colors are wheaten, red, black, or wolf-sable.

Size *Height:* 16–18in (40.5–46cm). *Weight:* 53–57lb (24–26kg).

Besides their normal work, Buhunds are also trained to aid people with defective hearing, perform some types of police work, and they score well in obedience and agility trials.

Characteristics and Temperament
Lively and alert, the Norwegian Buhund is a little reserved with strangers but friendly toward its family. Being extremely intelligent by nature, consistent training is needed from early puppyhood. The dog does not have a big appetite and has a coat that is easy to groom and keep clean.

OLD ENGLISH SHEEPDOG

Another of the almost universally recognized breeds of dog, the Old English Sheepdog, or Bobtail as it is also known, probably originated from crossings between European and British sheepdogs over 150 years ago. The breed's coat is its most distinctive feature – indeed, there is little else to be seen of th dog unless the coat has been clipped. This breed has gone from being a working dog to a highly popular pet and advertising icon, perhaps to the detriment of its original type.

Appearance A strong, symmetrical, square dog. The head has a rather square skull and a strong, square muzzle. The nose is black.

The eyes may be dark, wall-eyed or sometimes blue. Ears are small and carried close to the sides of the head. The neck is fairly long and arched. The short, compact body, with its muscular loins, is carried on long, strongly-boned legs. The tail is usually completely docked.

Coat Hard-textured and profuse, free from curl but shaggy, with a waterproof undercoat. Colors are gray, grizzle or blue in any shade; head, neck, forequarters and underbelly are white, with or without markings.

Size *Height:* male 24in (61cm) minimum; female 22in (56cm) minimum. *Weight:* male 80.5lb (36.5kg); female 65lb (29.5kg).

In the Old English Sheepdog, the herding instinct, that has been carried down through the generations, is still astonishingly strong, and they have been known not only to herd livestock but also members of their human family, pushing them away from dangerous objects.

Characteristics and Temperament
Old English Sheepdogs make intelligent, intuitive and loving companions, even earning the title 'babysitter' or 'nanny' when around young children. The breed needs plenty of exercise, and careful, regular grooming is required to avoid the coat from becoming hopelessly matted. The dog walks with a bear-like gait but moves freely and effortlessly at speed.

PINSCHER

This is a clean-looking, medium-sized dog of German origin, with an appearance reminiscent of a small Dobermann. The German Kennel Club recognized the breed in 1879. The dog is also known as the Standard Pinscher, the word Pinscher meaning 'terrier,' but this dog is too long-legged to go to earth, and is used for other duties, such as watchdog. Descended from early European herding and guardian breeds, the Pinscher is not related to the superficially similar terriers of Great Britain.

Appearance A smooth-coated, elegant, dog. The head has a moderately wide skull and a deep muzzle. The nose is black. The eyes are oval, dark and of medium size and with a lively expression. The ears are V-shaped and usually folded, although sometimes they are cropped. The neck is elegant and well-muscled. The body has a deep chest and is carried on strong, medium-length legs. The tail is usually docked.

Coat Short, dense and glossy. Solid colors, from fawn to red, or black and blue with red or tan markings, are commonly seen.

Size *Height:* 17–19in (43–48cm). *Weight:* 25–35lb (11.5–16kg).

Characteristics and Temperament A neat and nimble dog, the Pinscher is easy to groom and inexpensive to feed. Obedient, lively and friendly with those it knows, its wariness of strangers makes it a useful guard dog.

The Pinscher gained full acceptance by the American Kennel Club in 2003.

POLISH LOWLAND SHEEPDOG

With an ancestry that is believed to include the Hungarian Puli and long-coated herding dogs, the Polish Lowland Sheepdog has been in existence since at least the 16th century, when Polish sailors visiting British seaports are thought to have exchanged these dogs for native ones, and so helped the breed to spread. The Polish Lowland Sheepdog almost became extinct after the Second World War, but was saved by the efforts of a Polish vet, who bred from some of the few remaining examples.

Appearance A chunky, muscular, long-coated breed, reminiscent of the Bearded Collie. The head has a fairly broad, slightly arched skull with a muzzle equal in length to the skull. The nose should be as dark as possible. The eyes are hazel or brown and have an alert expression. The moderately large drop ears are heart-shaped. The neck

The Polish Lowland Sheepdog is partly descended from the Puli, but some time before the 16th century, other blood was introduced, most likely that of Hun herding dogs, there being evidence of the PON, as it now appears, in both Poland and Pomerania.

is muscular and strong. The body is rectangular in side view with a level back and muscular loins and is carried on well-muscled legs. The tail is usually docked, although some dogs are born tailless.

Coat The long, thick and shaggy outercoat has a hard texture; the undercoat is soft; the eyes are almost totally covered by long hair. Any color, but white, gray, and brown are most common, with black, gray, or brown markings. It is common for colors to fade as the dogs reach maturity.

Size *Height:* male 17–20in (43–51cm); female 16–18.5in (40.5–47cm). *Weight:* 43lb (19.5kg).

Characteristics and Temperament
This is a lively, intelligent and friendly dog that seems particularly fond of children.

The Polish Lowland Sheepdog needs plenty of exercise to help burn off some of its exuberant excess energy, but rewards its owner by being easy to train and happy to act as a dutiful watchdog. The long, thick coat requires regular and careful grooming.

PORTUGUESE WATER DOG

This dog probably arrived in Portugal with Moorish traders from North Africa. For centuries, the breed's great love of water has been put to good use by Portuguese fishermen, who use the dog for salvaging tackle and nets from the sea and for guarding the boats. Webbed feet help the dog to swim. The dog comes in two different coat-types – a long, wavy coat and a shorter, curly coat. The coat is usually clipped short over the hindquarters and most of the tail.

Appearance A rectangular, muscular dog reminiscent of a Poodle. The head has a long skull and a strong, slightly-tapering muzzle. The eyes are round and are dark brown or black in color. The drop ears are heart-shaped. The neck is short and straight and is carried on a short, deep-chested body. The long legs are well-boned and muscular and end in webbed feet. The tail is long and tapering and is carried in a ring-shaped arch over the back; a plume of hair is usually left on the end of the tail after the rest has been clipped.

Coat *Long-coated:* Thick and loosely waved; fairly glossy. *Short-coated:* Harsh and dense with tight curls; not glossy. The coat is clipped into characteristic style. Colors are black, white, brown, black-and-white, or brown-and-white.

Size *Height:* male 19.5–22.5in (49.5–57cm); female 17–20.5in (43–52cm). *Weight:* male 42–55lb (19–25kg); female 35–48lb (16–22kg).

Characteristics and Temperament The Portuguese Water Dog is cheerful, intelligent and energetic, with an excellent swimming ability. The breed can be obstinate, and therefore needs firm and consistent training.

Portuguese Water Dogs once rode the fishing trawlers, as they worked their way from the warm Atlantic waters of Portugal to the frigid fishing waters off the coast of Iceland, where the fleet caught saltwater codfish to bring back home.

PYRENEAN MOUNTAIN DOG

For centuries, this large and impressive dog was used to guard flocks against wolves, bears and other predators in the Pyrenees region of France and Spain. A descendant of the herding and guardian breeds of southern Europe, the breed was a favorite with French noblemen, and was named the Royal Dog of France by Louis XIV. In the Second World War, the Pyrenean was used as a pack dog and messenger by French troops. Today, it is a popular companion dog. It is also known as the Great Pyrenees in the US.

Appearance Strong, well-balanced and elegant. The head has a broad, fairly-arched skull and a medium-length, slightly tapering muzzle. The nose is black. The almond-shaped eyes have a thoughtful expression and are dark amber in color. The ears are triangular and lie at the sides of the head when the dog is resting. The neck is thick and muscular. The chest is broad and deep and the back is broad and muscular.

Great Pyrenees are related to several other large, white European livestock guardian dogs, including the Italian Maremma Sheepdog, the Hungarian Kuvasz, the Turkish Akbash, and the Tatra Sheepdog of Poland.

The legs are heavily boned and well-muscled, as befits such a powerful dog; the double dew-claws help the dog to tackle the mountainous terrain. The tail tapers toward the tip and is carried with the tip slightly curled.

Coat The outercoat is fairly long, coarse and thick; the undercoat is profuse; the coat forms a mane around the neck and shoulders. Colors are white, or white with patches of badger, wolf-gray or pale yellow.

Size *Height:* male 28in (71cm) minimum; female 26in (66cm) minimum.

Weight: male 110lb (50kg) minimum; female 90lb (41kg) minimum.

Characteristics and Temperament
The Pyrenean Mountain Dog is confident, kindly and dignified, but like any big dog needs correct handling. It makes a good companion for those who understand its

emotional needs, and mindful of what this dog was bred to do, an equally strong character is required to fully master it. The breed only requires average exercise and is likely to amble about rather than take off at speed. Despite its abundant coat, the Pyrenean only requires minimal care, as dirt and debris are readily shaken off.

PYRENEAN SHEEPDOG

This much smaller dog from the Pyrenees, used for herding flocks of sheep, probably originated from crosses between indigenous Pyrenean breeds and others, such as Briards. The breed is a fairly new arrival in Britain, and only received Kennel Club recognition in 1988. The coat may be long or semi-long.

Appearance A small, active, rough-coated sheepdog. The head has a fairly flat skull and a short, slightly tapering muzzle. The almond-shaped eyes look keen and alert; they are usually dark brown, although one or both may be blue or blue-flecked in merle or slate-colored dogs. The ears are fairly short. The neck is medium to long, and is carried on a lean, strong body with slightly arched loins. The legs are lean but well-muscled; the hind legs may have single or double dew-claws. The tail is medium-length with a slight hook at the tip; the tail may be docked, and some individuals may be born with only a stump.

Coat Rather hard and dense, flat or wavy. Colors are fawn, light to dark gray, blue merle, slate blue or brindle, black, or black-and-white.

Size *Height:* male 16–19in (40.5–48cm); female 15–18in (38–46cm). *Weight:* 18–33lb (8–15kg).

Characteristics and Temperament
Full of energy and stamina, the Pyrenean makes a good watchdog. They are 'one-man' dogs, attached and dedicated to their owners, having a desire to follow them around which makes them easy to train.

The Pyrenean Sheepdog come from the French side of the Pyrenees.

ROTTWEILER

The name of this dog was taken from the Roman settlement of Rottweil in Germany. When the Roman Empire was invading Germany, mastiff-type dogs were brought along too, for guarding and herding livestock. In time, Rottweil became an important trading center for cattle and other livestock, and butchers in the town used the dog for various duties including pulling carts. The breed's natural guarding instincts and boldness has made it a popular dog for use by police forces and other similar organizations. The Rottweiler first appeared in Britain in the 1930s and is one of the most popular dogs in America.

Overbreeding produced some poor examples, but this problem has now been largely overcome.

Appearance A compact, powerful and well-proportioned dog. The head has a wide, medium-length skull and a deep, broad muzzle. The nose is black. The brown eyes are almond-shaped. The ears are small and pendent. The neck is strong, round and very muscular. The body has a broad, deep chest with a straight, strong back. The legs are well-boned and muscular. The tail is normally docked at the first joint.

Coat The outercoat is medium-length, coarse and flat; the undercoat should not be visible through the outercoat. Color is black, with well-defined tan markings on cheeks, muzzle, chest, legs, over the eyes and under the tail.

Size *Height:* male 25–27in (63.5–68.5cm); female 23–25in (58.5–63.5cm). *Weight:* male 110lb (50kg); female 85lb (38.5kg).

Characteristics and Temperament
Bold, loyal and courageous, the Rottweiler is also an active dog that likes plenty of

The Rottweiler is a self-assured and well-balanced dog, but early socialization and exposure to as many new people, animals, and situations as possible is very important in developing these qualities. The Rottweiler also has a natural tendency to assert dominance if it is not correctly trained.

exercise. The short coat responds well to grooming, and a splendid sheen is easy to produce. This is a willing worker and an excellent guard dog, but proper handling and training are essential requirements for ownership of such a characterful dog.

St. Bernard

It would be difficult to mistake the St. Bernard for any other dog, for this gentle giant is depicted everywhere as a symbol of rescue and care. A descendant of mastiff-type dogs brought to the Swiss Alps by the Romans over 2,000 years ago, the dog achieved fame when it was used by the monks at the Hospice of St. Bernard for rescuing travelers lost in the St. Gothard Pass. The dog comes in two coat-types: rough-coated and smooth-coated.

Appearance A well-proportioned, massive dog of substance. The huge head has a broad, slightly rounded skull and a short, deep muzzle. The nose is black. The dark eyes are medium-sized and should have a benevolent expression. The triangular ears are medium-sized and lie close to the cheeks. The neck is thick and muscular with a well-developed dewlap. The deep-chested body has a straight back and muscular loins and is carried on straight, heavily-boned legs. The feet are large, which no doubt help the dog to progress through snow. The tail is long.

Coat *Rough-coated:* Flat and dense and full around the neck. *Smooth-coated:* Close-fitting and hound-like with feathering on the thighs and tail. Colors are orange, mahogany-brindle, red-brindle, or white with patches on the body of any of these colors.

Size *Height:* male 28in (71cm) minimum; female 26in (66cm) minimum. *Weight:* male 165.5lb (75kg); female 150lb (68kg).

Characteristics and Temperament Fortunately, this massive dog has an extremely equable temperament and a steady, calm nature. Walks are usually taken at a leisurely pace, but a St. Bernard can pull extremely hard, so needs to be kept under control. Around the house, they are inclined to drool and are not one of those large breeds that can curl up into surprisingly small spaces – an owner tends to fit around whatever space is left. Feeding is also an expensive business.

Extremely loyal and a good watchdog, the St. Bernard is always eager to please its owner, but it is essential, due to its great bulk, that correct training and socialization begin early in life while the dog is still a manageable size.

SAMOYED

The Samoyed was originally used to guard the reindeer herds and pull the sleds of the wandering tribesmen of the Siberian tundra. Fur traders brought the breed back to Britain, and Samoyeds were also used on a number of polar expeditions.

Appearance A well-proportioned, graceful, Spitz-type dog with a sparkling, stand-off coat. The head is wedge-shaped with a wide skull and a medium-length muzzle. The nose is black, brown or flesh-colored. The brown eyes are almond-shaped, enhancing the 'laughing' expression so characteristic of this dog. The ears are thick, with slightly rounded tips, and are held erect. The strong neck is carried on a broad, muscular body with a deep chest. The legs are very muscular and well-boned. The tail is held curled over the back and to one side.

Coat A thick, close, short undercoat and a harsh, straight outercoat which grows away from the body giving protection from the cold. Colors are pure white, white-and-biscuit, and cream.

Size *Height:* male 20–22in (51–56cm); female 18–20in (46–51cm). *Weight:* male 50.5lb (23kg); female 39.5lb (18kg).

An aggressive Samoyed is a rarity, making it a poor watchdog, but it is known to be stubborn at times and difficult to train. Its heritage means that it is used to pulling a sled, and it is therefore not averse, when on a leash, to pulling its owner rather than walking correctly alongside.

Characteristics and Temperament
The Samoyed is a charming dog that loves human company. Fairly obedient in a rather laid-back way, the breed nevertheless enjoys life and lets everyone know it. The coat needs plenty of grooming, but the Samoyed is quite happy to submit to any amount of attention.

SHETLAND SHEEPDOG

The bleak Shetland Isles, off the north-east coast of Scotland, are the original home of this dog, which bears a strong resemblance to the Rough Collie. Although small, the breed was quite capable of working with the smaller Shetland ponies and other livestock of the area.

Appearance An elegant and symmetrical sheepdog, the head is in the shape of a blunt wedge. It has a flat, fairly broad skull and a long, rounded muzzle. The nose is black. The almond-shaped eyes are

obliquely set and are usually dark brown, although they may be blue or blue-flecked in merles. The small ears are usually carried semi-erect with the tips falling forward. The well-arched neck is carried on a deep-chested body with a level back. The muscular legs are moderately long. The tail is well-furred.

Coat The outercoat of long hair is hard and straight; the undercoat is soft and short; the hair forms an abundant mane and frill. Colors are sable, tricolor, blue merle, black-and-white, and black-and-tan.

Size *Height:* male 14.5in (37cm); female 14in (35.5cm). *Weight:* 20lb (9kg).

Characteristics and Temperament
This attractive little dog makes a good companion for people of all ages, being watchful, intelligent and active. The breed has undemanding feeding requirements, but the coat requires plenty of regular grooming to keep it looking good.

The Sheltie has brains as well as beauty and, like the Shetland Pony, has intentionally been bred small.

SIBERIAN HUSKY

The Siberian Husky was developed by the Chukchi peoples of Arctic northeast Asia as a fast, long-distance sled dog. Indeed, this is the fastest of all the sled-pulling breeds, and the dog seems happiest when performing this task. Although more lightly built than other sled dogs, the Siberian Husky is tough, strong and has good powers of endurance.

Appearance A purposeful, medium-sized sled dog. The head is rather fox-like, with a slightly rounded skull and a medium-length muzzle. The nose is black in gray, black or tan dogs, liver in copper-colored dogs, and flesh-colored in white individuals. The eyes are almond-shaped and may be brown or blue, or parti-colored. The triangular ears are held firmly erect. The neck is arched and is carried on a medium-length, muscular and deep-chested body. Well-muscled, powerful legs end in oval, slightly-webbed feet with fur between the toes. The tail has a fox-like brush.

Coat The outercoat is straight and smooth-lying; the undercoat is soft and dense. The coat may be of any color, including white.

Size *Height:* male 21–23in (53.5–58.5cm); female 20–22in (51–56cm). *Weight:* male 45–60lb (20.5–27kg); female 35–50lb (16–22.5kg).

Characteristics and Temperament
Friendly and extremely tolerant toward people, the same cannot always be said of the Siberian Husky's attitude to other dogs, which it will usually try to dominate. Indifferent to the coldest of weather, the breed is not a typical pet by any means. It will jump over almost anything, or dig under it, and will usually pull on the leash and then take off like a rocket when released. The breed is mostly kept for sled racing.

The Siberian Husky is not an ideal pet. It has a very dense coat and prefers to live outdoors.

WELSH CORGI (CARDIGAN)

Originally bred as a cattle dog, the Cardigan Welsh Corgi is the older of the two varieties of Welsh Corgi, with a history going back 800 years. Nevertheless, it is the least well-known of the two breeds. It is also the only one with a tail, and the Cardigan differs from the Pembroke in other respects, too, such as in coat-color, ear-length and foot-shape.

Appearance A sturdy, short-legged and active dog. The head has a fox-like shape with a wide, flat skull and a tapering muzzle. The nose is black. The eyes have an alert but kindly expression and should be dark, although one or both may be blue or blue-flecked in merles. The ears are proportionately large with rounded tips, widely-spaced and held erect. A muscular neck is carried on a long, fairly broad-chested body. The legs are short but strong, and the feet are round. The brush-like tail is long enough to touch the ground but is usually lifted when on the move.

Coat Weatherproof; short or slightly longer, and with a hard texture. Any colors are permitted.

Both the Cardigan and Pembroke Corgis are among the healthiest and longest-lived of the Herding group. The Cardigan tends to be a little hardier and has fewer documented hereditary health issues.

Size *Height:* 12in (30.5cm). *Weight:* 22–24lb (10–11kg).

Characteristics and Temperament
Active and fast-moving on occasions, the Cardigan Welsh Corgi can also take life at a steadier pace when it feels like it. Intelligent and obedient, the breed makes a good companion and watchdog.

WELSH CORGI (PEMBROKE)

The better-known of the two breeds of Welsh Corgi, this version usually has its tail docked. Another cattle-driving dog, the Pembroke also earned its keep by nipping at the heels of cattle to encourage them to move on – a trick that has also been played on people on occasions! This breed also has a long working history, as well as being the favorite pet of Queen Elizabeth II of England, who has owned many examples of this dog over the years.

Appearance A sturdy, short-legged and active dog. The head has a fox-like shape with a wide, flat skull and a tapering muzzle. The nose is black. The round eyes are brown in color. The ears are of medium size with rounded tips, widely-spaced and held erect. A fairly long, muscular neck is carried on a long, fairly broad-chested body. The legs are short but strong, and the feet are oval. The tail is usually docked.

Coat Weatherproof; short or slightly longer and with a hard texture. Colors are

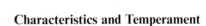

A house without either a cat or a dog is the house of a scoundrel.

Portuguese Proverb

red, sable, fawn, or black-and-tan, usually with white markings on the legs, neck, chest and face.

Size *Height:* 10–12in (25.5–30.5cm). *Weight:* 22–24lb (10–11kg).

Characteristics and Temperament

A popular and outgoing dog, the Pembroke makes a good companion for an active family. It likes nothing better than a good romp out in the open air, followed by a square meal. Its fondness for food should be moderated, however, to avoid obesity. It is an intelligent dog with a tendency toward dominance if given half a chance.

The Pembroke Corgi appears to be quite a hardy little dog but there are some ailments that are common to the breed, with a tendency to become overweight that can lead to back and joint problems.

CHAPTER SIX
TOY DOGS

Some groups – the Hounds, the Gundogs and the Terriers, for instance – comprise dogs sharing common characteristics. Within each of these groups, therefore, we find dogs with either an inbuilt tendency to hunt, or to retrieve, or to go to earth in pursuit of quarry. The Toy group also includes dogs that have one overriding characteristic in common – that of being small – even if they do come in a variety of different shapes. In this respect, therefore, the Toy group shares a common link with the aforementioned groups, yet it also has similarities with the Working Dog and Utility Dog groups, both of which also have a heterogeneous collection of breeds within their ranks.

The dogs in the Toy group are also bred with a different purpose in mind. Although many breeds within the other groups are kept solely as pets, their original purpose was to perform some kind of work or task. Toy dogs are bred primarily to be companions (although many of them also make excellent watchdogs and some can catch vermin very adequately).

Despite their small size, Toy dogs are still dogs, and they should be treated as such. They may not need to expend as much energy as some other breeds, but they

Despite its diminutive size, the Chihuahua is a spirited and intelligent dog that moves in a swift and purposeful way. It is friendly but will quickly raise the alarm at the approach of strangers to the door.

still need adequate amounts of exercise and a correct canine diet. Being carried around all day and fed sweets and other inappropriate food is a demeaning way to treat a dog. Given the chance, most Toy breeds will enjoy a romp in the open air and can normally give a good account of themselves when confronted by larger varieties of their species. A properly treated dog, whatever its size, will return the

kindness shown to it with affection and by being an amusing and stimulating companion. Most Toy breeds are highly intelligent and can quickly and easily be trained. Another feature shared by most of them is that they are attractive and neat-looking animals.

The Toy group has representatives drawn from many other breed-types, as well as some that are unique to the group. The terriers are represented in the form of the Australian Silky Terrier, the English Toy Terrier, and the Yorkshire Terrier, being dogs that, although small, have all the typical terrier characteristics of bravery and cheekiness.

For admirers of spaniels the choice includes the King Charles Spaniel and the Cavalier King Charles Spaniel, while lovers of Spitz-type dogs will find the Pomeranian has all the spark and energy – and the voice – of its larger cousins.

Exotic, long-coated dogs come no better than in the form of the Papillon and the Pekingese, and for grace and elegance it would be hard to find a better example than the Italian Greyhound – truly a Greyhound in miniature. And for sheer character and a look of pure mischief nothing can beat the Griffon Bruxellois.

Prepared for a show, groomed impeccably, and with bows in its hair, it is easy to forget that the Yorkie is a typical terrier, bred originally for work and still possessing all the pluckiness and spirit of the breed.

AFFENPINSCHER

There is some disagreement concerning the exact origins of the Affenpinscher, with some authorities believing it to be a descendant of wire-coated terrier types from Scandinavia, while others think it has a link with breeds from Asia. The dog in its present form comes from Germany, and has been known there for centuries, where it is also known as the Black Devil because of its mischievous expression.

Appearance A rough-coated, robust-looking dog with a monkey-like face, the head has a rather broad skull and a short, blunt muzzle. The nose is black. The dark, round eyes have a glint to them. The ears are small and may be drop or erect. The short neck is carried on a body with a

short, straight back. The legs are straight, and the tail is carried high.

Coat Short, dense, hard and wiry; the head has prominent whiskers. The coat-color is usually black, but there may also be gray in the coat.

Size *Height:* 9.5–11in (24–28cm). *Weight:* 6.5–9lb (3–4kg).

Characteristics and Temperament Full of character and energy, the Affenpinscher is a delightful small companion dog that will also fearlessly confront any uninvited visitor to its home.

The Affenpinscher is believed to have been a major influence in the development of many of the smaller, rough-coated breeds of continental Europe, including the Brussels Griffon and the Miniature Schnauzer. The area around Munich eventually became the center of Affenpinscher breeding in Europe.

AUSTRALIAN SILKY TERRIER

This breed came about in the 1800s as the result of crossings between the Yorkshire Terrier and the Australian Terrier. It was formerly known as the Sydney Silky Terrier, after a well-known breeder of these dogs moved to the city of that name with his kennels. In Europe, the dog is generally placed in the Terrier group.

Appearance A low-slung, long-coated dog with a refined look about it. The head is wedge-shaped, with a moderately broad, flat skull. The nose is black. The eyes are round, small, and have an alert expression. The ears are V-shaped and pricked. The

neck is slightly arched and is carried on a longish body. The legs are short and finely-boned. The tail is usually docked and is carried erect.

Coat Fine, straight, long and glossy with a silky texture. Colors are blue-and-tan, and gray-blue-and-tan.

Size *Height:* 9in (23cm). *Weight:* 9lb (4kg).

Characteristics and Temperament
Australian Silky Terriers are bred as house dogs, so tend to have a strong attachment to their owner, coupled with a slight suspicion of strangers and strange dogs. Once the visitor is welcomed by the owner, however, most will completely accept the visitor and vie for attention from them. The generally elegant appearance of this breed should not disguise the fact that the Silky is a real terrier!

The Australian Silky Terrier has all its terrier instincts intact, despite its diminutive size. It is a lively little dog with plenty of stamina.

BICHON FRISÉ

This sprightly little dog, a small breed of the Bichon type, is similar in appearance to, but larger than the Maltese Bichon. It originated in the Mediterranean region, possibly as long ago as the 14th century. Later, it found favor in the royal courts of Europe, and after the French Revolution became a familiar part of circus acts. But by the 19th century, its popularity had declined, although the breed's fortunes were restored when it was recognized by the French Kennel Club in 1934.

Appearance A sturdy, lively little dog with a thick woolly coat. The head has a broad skull with a shortish muzzle. The nose is black. The eyes are large, dark and round; their expression is one of alertness. The ears are pendulous. An arched, moderately-long neck is carried on a body with a well-developed chest and broad loins. The legs are straight and well-boned. The tail is usually carried in a curve over the back.

Coat Thick, silky and loosely curled; the coat is often clipped into a distinctive shape. The color should be solid white.

Bichon Frisés are high-maintenance, requiring regular, expensive, and time-consuming grooming. An alternative is a shorter 'puppy cut' which, when done properly, can eliminate daily grooming.

Size *Height:* 9–11in (23–28cm). *Weight:* 6.5–13lb (3–6kg).

Characteristics and Temperament
Lively and confident, the Bichon Frisé enjoys receiving plenty of attention from its owner. It likes to join in family games and requires little exercise.

CAVALIER KING CHARLES SPANIEL

The more people I meet the more I like my dog.

Anonymous

This dog has been known for several hundred years and was popular at European courts in the 17th century. Larger than its relative the King Charles Spaniel, and with a nose that is less snub, the Cavalier King Charles Spaniel achieved recognition as a breed in the 1940s.

Appearance An attractive, well-balanced small spaniel. The head has a flattish skull and a short, square muzzle. The nose is black. The large, round eyes are dark in color and have a trusting expression that is most endearing. The ears are long and pendulous, with ample feathering. The neck is of medium length and slightly arched. The body is short with a level back and is carried on moderately boned legs. The tail is fairly long, although sometimes it is docked by one third.

Coat Long and silky and sometimes with a slight wave and good feathering. Colors are black-and-tan, ruby (rich red), Blenheim (chestnut-and-white) or tricolor (black, white and tan).

Size *Height:* 13in (33cm). *Weight:* 12–18lb (5.5–8kg).

Characteristics and Temperament
One of the most popular of the Toy breeds, the Cavalier King Charles seems to have everything to offer as a companion, in that it is friendly, happy to run in the fields or sit by its owner's side, is built like a proper sporting dog, and is easy to feed and groom.

Some Cavaliers seem to have traits in common with cats, in that they perch in high places, clean their own paws, and have even been seen to catch low-flying birds in mid-flight.

233

CHIHUAHUA

This dog gets its name from the Mexican state of Chihuahua where, around the mid-1890s, it first became well-known to the Western world – although there is evidence that it may have actually originated from the Orient. Soon after, the dog was introduced into the United States, where the breed standard was improved. The American and UK Kennel Clubs recognize only two types of Chihuahua: the smooth-coated and the long-coated forms. This is generally considered to be the world's smallest breed of dog.

Appearance Tiny and neat-looking, the dog has a prominent head with a broad, rounded skull and a short, pointed muzzle with a distinct stop. The large, round eyes are set well apart, the color varying according to coat-color. The distinctive ears are large and flared and set at the sides of the head. The slightly arched neck is carried on an elongated body with a level back. Legs are medium-length and moderately well-boned. The tail is carried over the back.

Coat *Smooth-coated:* Smooth, soft and glossy. *Long-coated:* Soft, and flat or wavy; feathering on feet, legs and ruff. Any colors are permissible.

Chihuahuas are prized as something of a curiosity. Their size makes them easily adaptable to a variety of environments, including small city apartments.

Size *Height:* 6–9in (15–23cm). *Weight:* 2–6lb (1–3kg).

Characteristics and Temperament
Despite its diminutive size, the Chihuahua is a spirited and intelligent dog that moves with a swift and purposeful action. It is friendly but will raise the alarm at the approach of unknown visitors. Although undemanding to feed, groom and exercise, it is unsuitable around small children.

CHINESE CRESTED DOG

A favorite dog of the Han Dynasty in China, the Chinese Crested was used to guard treasure and even in some forms of hunting. The dog was first shown in America in 1885. The breed comes in two coat-forms: the Hairless (with a crest of hair on the head, with hair covering parts of the legs and feet and with a plume of hair on the tail), and the Powderpuff (with a body covered in fine hair).

Appearance An active and graceful dog, the head has a moderately broad, elongated skull and a medium-to-long, tapering muzzle. The nose may be any color. The almond-shaped eyes are almost black and are set widely apart. The large ears are held erect in the Hairless variety, but drop ears are permitted in the Powderpuff. The neck is long and lean. The body is of medium length with a deep chest. The legs are long and lightly-boned, ending in hare-like feet. The tail is long and tapering.

Coat *Hairless:* Hair is confined to head-crest, lower legs and feet and tail plume; the skin may be plain or spotted and may lighten in summer. *Powderpuff:* Coat consists of a soft veil of long hair. Any color is permitted.

Size *Height:* 9–13in (23–33cm); *Weight:* 12lb (5.5kg).

Characteristics and Temperament
Happy, lively and affectionate, the Chinese Crested Dog is a tough breed that enjoys reasonable amounts of exercise. The Hairless is at risk of sunburn, and should be protected whenever it goes outside.

The Chinese Crested possibly evolved from African hairless dogs, which were traded among merchants, making their way to ancient ports around the world. The Chinese, who seemed to favor smaller dogs, selectively bred this dog to an even smaller size.

235

ENGLISH TOY TERRIER

The English Toy Terrier, once known as the Toy Black-and-Tan Terrier, has an ancestry which includes the now-extinct British black-and-tan terrier. During Regency and Georgian periods, the English Toy was a familiar sight in rat pits, where the active little dog would work against the clock, with wagers having been placed on the number of rats it could kill in the allotted time.

Appearance A well-balanced, elegant and compact dog, reminiscent of a small, prick-eared Manchester Terrier. The head has a long, flat and narrow skull and a narrowing muzzle. The nose is black. The almond-shaped eyes are small and dark with a bright and lively expression. The ears are held erect by the time the dog is mature, and are described as 'candle-flame' in shape. The long, arched neck is carried on a short body with a slightly curving back and a deep, narrow chest. The legs are long and fine-boned. The tail is long and tapering.

Coat Thick, close, smooth and glossy. Color is black-and-tan; the breed standard is very precise concerning the distribution of the tan markings.

Size *Height:* 10–12in (25.5–30.5cm). *Weight:* 6–8lb (3–3.5kg).

While the name English Toy Terrier is sometimes used synonymously with that of the Toy Manchester Terrier, these are actually separate breeds. The English Toy is on the UK Kennel Club's list of vulnerable native breeds and great effort is being made to boost the popularity of the breed and develop a viable gene pool.

Characteristics and Temperament
A sound example of this breed moves with a smooth, flowing action and is a delight to watch. The English Toy Terrier has all the characteristics of a true terrier, including alertness, speed of movement, and is a talented rodent-hunter. It is also friendly and typically courageous.

GRIFFON BRUXELLOIS

This dog comes from Belgium, where it was used in stables for keeping down rodents and for raising the alarm if anyone approached. Dogs very similar to the Griffon Bruxellois were depicted in paintings in the 1400s, and the breed was well-established in the 1600s. There is a mixture of breeds in its ancestry, including the Affenpinscher, Pug and various terriers. Two varieties exist – a rough-coated form and a smooth-coated form known as the Petit Brabançon.

Appearance A square, well-built little dog with a monkey-like face. The head has a broad, round skull, a short, wide muzzle and a prominent chin. The nose is black.

The eyes are large and round. The ears are semi-erect. The medium-length neck is

slightly arched, and the deep-chested body is carried on straight, medium-length legs. The tail is usually docked.

Coat *Rough-coated:* Hard and wiry, but not curly; a prominent walrus mustache. *Smooth-coated:* Short and tight. Color types are as follows: Griffon Bruxellois: Red or reddish-brown, with black allowed on muzzle; Griffon Belge: Black, black-and-tan, black-and-red, which may have a black face mask; Petit Brabançon: the same colors as for the preceding two.

Size *Height:* 7–8in (18–20.5cm). *Weight:* 5–11lb (2.5–5kg).

Characteristics and Temperament
Griffons must not be shy or aggressive; however, they are emotionally sensitive, and should be socialized carefully at a young age. Griffons should also be alert, inquisitive, and interested in their surroundings.

The US saw a surge of interest in the breed, due to the appearance of a Griffon in the 1997 movie, As Good As It Gets.

ITALIAN GREYHOUND

Dogs very similar in appearance to this breed can be seen depicted in the tombs of ancient pharaohs, although the modern Italian Greyhound was probably bred in more recent Roman times. This is the smallest of the sighthounds, and its diminutive size precludes serious chasing as part of a hunt. Instead, it is admired for its small-scale elegance, ease of maintenance, and gentle nature.

Appearance A Greyhound in miniature, the head has a long, flat, narrow skull and a

fine, long muzzle. The nose may be any dark color. Eyes are expressive, large and bright. The delicate, rose-shaped ears are set well back on the head. The long neck is gracefully arched, carried on a narrow, deep-chested body; the back is slightly arched over the loins. The legs are long and well-muscled and end in hare-like feet. The tail is long and fine, and carried low.

Coat Satin-like, fine and short. Colors are black, blue, cream, fawn, red, white – or any of these colors with white.

Size *Height:* 13–15in (33–38cm). *Weight:* 6–10lb (3–4.5kg).

Characteristics and Temperament
Despite its fragile appearance, the Italian Greyhound is brave, energetic, and also affectionate. It has a good turn of speed, covering the ground with the same long-striding gait as its larger cousins.

As gazehounds, Italian Greyhounds instinctively hunt by sight and have a high predatory drive. To prevent them breaking away and chasing after smaller animals, keep them on the leash when out in the open air.

JAPANESE CHIN

This attractive little dog is also known as the Japanese Spaniel, although it has a strong resemblance to the Pekingese. The breed probably arrived in Japan as a gift from the Chinese royal court.

Appearance A lively and dainty little dog with a distinctive face. The head is large with a broad skull, rounded in front, and with a short, wide muzzle and deep stop. The nose is usually black, but in reds and whites it may be of a color harmonizing with the coat. The eyes are large and dark and set widely apart. The small, V-shaped ears are well-feathered. The body is compact with a broad chest and is carried on straight, fine-boned legs ending in hare-like feet. The tail is well-feathered and carried curved over the back.

Coat Long, silky, soft, straight and profuse. Colors are black-and-white or red-and-white.

Size *Height:* 7in (18cm). *Weight:* 4–7lb (2–3kg).

The Chin has cat-like traits, using its paws to wash its face, and resting on the backs of sofas and chairs. It can also walk across a table without disturbing objects resting on it.

Characteristics and Temperament
The Japanese Chin is a tiny dog with a cheerful and friendly nature, the breed's characteristic facial expression being one suggesting surprise. Although happy to go for leisurely walks, it is unfair to expect it to undertake anything too demanding. The coat needs regular grooming to keep it in good condition.

KING CHARLES SPANIEL

Also known as the English Toy Spaniel, the King Charles Spaniel is so named because it was a favorite at the court of the English king, Charles II. Many paintings from the period also depict one or more of these spaniels somewhere in the scene, such was their popularity. This spaniel is closely related to the Cavalier King Charles Spaniel. The King Charles Spaniel, however, has a shorter nose and a slightly more domed skull than the Cavalier.

Appearance A cobby and aristocratic-looking small dog. The head has a broad, arched skull and a short, square, upturned muzzle. The nose is black. The eyes are large, set widely apart, and have a friendly expression. The well-feathered ears are long and pendulous. The arched neck is carried on a broad, deep-chested body. The legs are short and straight. The tail, also well-feathered, may be docked.

Coat Long, silky and straight. Colors are black-and-tan, ruby (rich red), Blenheim (chestnut-and-white) or tricolor (black, white and tan).

Size *Height:* male 10in (25.5cm); female 8in (20.5cm). *Weight:* 8–14lb (3.5–6.5kg).

The King Charles Spaniel was recognized in North America as the English Toy Spaniel, presumably to avoid confusing it with the Cavalier King Charles Spaniel. The AKC has two classes: English Toy Spaniel (Blenheim Prince Charles) and English Toy Spaniel (Ruby King Charles).

Characteristics and Temperament
An appealing small dog with a gentle and affectionate nature, the King Charles Spaniel is undemanding both in terms of feeding and exercise. It is a bright and interested little dog that is always willing to please.

LÖWCHEN (LITTLE LION DOG)

The Löwchen has been known in European countries, such as France, Spain and Germany, since the 1500s. By 1960, however, the popularity of the Löwchen had declined to such an extent that it was listed as the rarest dog in the world – although numbers have improved since then – and the breed has continued to gain new fans. This bichon-type breed gets its other name, Little Lion, because of the characteristic lion-like shape into which its coat is sometimes trimmed.

Appearance A well-built, active dog with a coat clipped into a shape resembling that of a lion. The head is short and broad with a flat skull, a short, strong muzzle, and a well-defined stop. The eyes are large and round, conveying intelligence. The ears are pendent. The body is short and strong and is carried on strong, straight legs. The tail is of medium length and is clipped into a tuft of hair at the end, resembling a plume.

Coat Long and wavy. Any coat-color is permitted.

Together with the Portuguese Water Dog and the Havanese, the Löwchen has also been called the rarest dog in the world and the breed still has only a few hundred new registrations each year throughout the world.

Size *Height:* 10–13in (25.5–33cm). *Weight:* 6.5lb (3kg).

Characteristics and Temperament
A friendly, lively and intelligent little dog, the Löwchen makes a good family pet and is robust enough to enjoy boisterous games with children.

MALTESE

The Maltese, or Maltese Terrier, is one of the oldest breeds in Europe. It was probably introduced to Malta by Phenicians, trading around the Mediterranean, and there is evidence of the dog being admired by early civilizations, such as the ancient Greeks. The Romans also kept these small dogs as pets, and they became popular again in the Middle Ages.

Appearance A neat little dog with a profuse white coat. The head has a flat skull and a short, broad muzzle. The nose is black. The eyes are dark brown, producing an intelligent expression. The ears are long, well-feathered and pendulous. The body is short and cobby and carried on short, straight legs. The tail, also well-feathered, is carried arched over the back.

Coat Long, straight and silky. The color should be pure white, although occasional lemon markings sometimes appear.

Size *Height:* 10in (25.5cm). *Weight:* 4–6lb (2–3kg).

Characteristics and Temperament
The Maltese moves with a free-flowing action, seeming to glide along with its coat wafting around it. Although small, this is a tough, friendly and alert dog that likes to play and enjoys exercise. The coat needs plenty of grooming to keep it in peak condition.

Maltese have no undercoats, and there is little to no shedding of the coat if it is cared for properly. Like the Poodle and Bichon Frisé, they are considered to be largely hypoallergenic, and many people who are allergic to dogs may find they are not allergic to the Maltese.

MINIATURE PINSCHER

A German breed, the Miniature Pinscher, as the name suggests, is the smallest of the Pinscher-type dogs. Also known as the 'King of the Toy Dogs,' the Miniature was bred from German terriers about 100 years ago, and is now widely popular.

Appearance A compact, elegant, smooth-coated small dog. The head is long with a flat skull and a strong muzzle. The nose is usually black, but in blue- or chocolate-coated dogs it may harmonize with the coat-color. The eyes are usually black. The ears may be carried erect or in the half-dropped position. The neck is graceful and arched and carried on a short, moderately deep-chested body. The legs are straight and medium-boned. The tail may be docked short or left as it is; if left

intact, the tail is often carried arched over the body.

Coat Smooth, straight, hard and glossy. Colors are black, blue, chocolate with tan markings, or various shades of red.

Size *Height:* 10–12in (25.5–30.5cm). *Weight:* 7.5lb (3.5kg).

Characteristics and Temperament
Although small, the Miniature Pinscher is a fearless, active and alert dog, and moves with a characteristic, high-stepping gait. It also has good hearing and will bark to alert the household when strangers approach.

The white gene is part of the breed's makeup although efforts have been made to eliminate it from the coat. White is accepted by the AKC, as long as it is limited to no more than half an inch in either direction.

PAPILLON

The Papillon, also known as the Butterfly Dog because of the shape of its ears, is recognized as a Franco-Belgian breed. In fact, there are two versions of this dog – one with erect ears (the origin of the name 'Papillon') and the other with drop ears. Once popular in the royal courts of Europe, the dog is much admired today.

Appearance An alert, silky-coated dog. The head has a slightly rounded skull and a pointed muzzle with a well-defined stop. The nose is black. The medium-sized eyes are dark and alert. The ears are of two types: either erect and held like the open wings of a butterfly, or carried dropped; in either style the ears are well-fringed with hair. The body is long, with a level back, and is carried on finely-boned legs that end in hare-like feet. The long tail is arched over the back and falls to one side.

Coat Full, flowing, long and silky; the chest has a profuse frill. The coat is white with patches of any color except liver; the preferred markings on the head include a white stripe down the center of the skull that helps to accentuate the butterfly effect.

There are two ear variations, the completely upright ears of the more common Papillon, and the dropped spaniel-like ears of the Phalène. The AKC and FCI consider the Phalène and the Papillon to be the same breed.

Size *Height:* 8–11in (20.5–28cm). *Weight:* 7.5lb (3.5kg).

Characteristics and Temperament
Intelligent, affectionate and easy to train, the Papillon is a star performer in obedience tests. The dog is a delightful pet, but is not recommended for small children.

PEKINGESE

Once the sacred dog of China and named after the capital city of that country, this is another of those breeds that are recognized the world over. Its ancestry can be traced at least back to the 8th-century Tang Dynasty, and for centuries the Pekingese was highly prized at the Imperial court. Perhaps this royal patronage explains something of the sense of self-importance that the Pekingese seems to convey. In the 1860s, some examples of the breed were brought to England after Peking (Beijing) was overrun, and in the early 1900s it was introduced to America.

Appearance A small, well-balanced and long-coated dog with a characteristic monkey face. The head is large, with a broad skull and a short, broad, wrinkled muzzle with a strong under-jaw. The flat nose is black. The eyes are large and round. The ears are heart-shaped and pendulous. The short neck is carried on a short body with a broad chest. The short legs are well-boned, the hind legs being somewhat lighter. The well-feathered tail is carried tightly curled over one side of the back.

Coat Long and thick with a full mane and good feathering on the ears, legs, tail and feet; the outercoat is coarse and there is a thick undercoat. All colors are permitted except liver and albino.

Size *Height:* 7in (18cm). *Weight:* male 11lb (5kg); female 12lb (5.5kg).

Characteristics and Temperament
Playful and fearless, the Pekingese is also an affectionate dog that makes a highly individual pet. However, this is not a breed that takes kindly to long walks in the country, preferring to amble along at its own pace with its characteristic rolling gait. The coat needs plenty of regular grooming to keep it in peak condition.

The Empress Dowager Cixi (1861–1908) was the de facto ruler of the Manchu Qing Dynasty, and she presented Pekingese dogs to several Americans, including John Pierpont Morgan and Alice Lee Roosevelt Longworth, the daughter of Theodore Roosevelt. Alice appropriately named her Pekingese, Manchu.

POMERANIAN

This is the smallest of the Spitz-type dogs and is a descendant of the large sled-pulling dogs of the Arctic region. This German dog came to Britain in the late 1870s, and its popularity later received a boost when Queen Victoria decide to keep examples of the breed.

Appearance A small, compact, fox-faced dog with a profuse coat. The head has a slightly flat skull and a short, pointed muzzle. The nose is black in white, sable or orange dogs, brown in chocolate-tipped sable dogs, and self-colored in dogs with other coat-colors. The eyes are bright and dark with an intelligent expression. The ears are small and held erect. The body is short, with a deep chest, and is carried on

finely-boned, medium-length legs. The tail is carried over the back in Spitz fashion.

Coat The outercoat is long, straight and harsh, and very thick around the neck and shoulders; the undercoat is soft and thick. All colors are permitted, including white, black, cream, brown, orange, beaver and sable.

Size *Height:* 8.5–11in (21.5–28cm). *Weight:* male 4–4.5lb (1.8–2kg); female 4.5–5.5lb (2–2.5kg).

Characteristics and Temperament Pomeranians have plenty of energy like their larger cousins. Extroverted and vivacious, it also has a shrill bark to alert its owner of approaching strangers.

The FCI classifies the German Spitz as one family, consisting of the Dwarf (Pomeranian), Small (American Eskimo Dog) and Standard (Wolfspitz/Keeshond).

248

PUG

The Pug is thought to have originated in China, where the dog was the companion of monks. It arrived in Europe with traders in the 1500s and subsequently became very popular in the Netherlands and in Britain.

Appearance A square, muscular dog reminiscent of a miniature mastiff. The head is large and round with a short, blunt muzzle; the skin has clearly-defined wrinkles. The huge, dark eyes are set in the sockets in a way that makes them seem globular; the eyes are also highly expressive.

The ears are small and thin, and there are two types: drop rose ears or folded button ears – the latter are preferred. The neck is strong and thick and is carried on a short, wide-chested body. The fairly long legs are strong and straight. The tail is curled tightly over the hip.

Coat Short, smooth, soft and glossy. Colors are silver, fawn, apricot or black; light colors should have clearly contrasting markings, including a dark mask and ears.

Size *Height:* 10–11in (25.5–28cm). *Weight:* 14–18lb (6.5–8kg).

Bred to be the lap-dogs of Chinese emperors during the Shang dynasty (1600-1046 BC), the dogs could be seen transmogrified into dragons with bulging eyes in painted artefacts. The Pug's popularity spread to Tibet, where it was kept mainly by monks, then spread to Japan, and finally Europe.

Characteristics and Temperament
The sturdy Pug is a real character among dogs. The body language and the almost talking eyes can express all manner of moods from alert watchfulness to an appealing request for attention. A playful dog, the Pug enjoys exercise and is easy to feed and groom.

YORKSHIRE TERRIER

The Yorkie's ancestors were most probably Clydesdale, Paisley, Skye and Waterside Terriers, and the Bitish black-and-tan terrier bloodline probably gave it its signature color-pattern. It first came to prominence in the 1850s, having been bred for ratting, bearing in mind that the breed was then larger than it is today.

Appearance A compact, long-coated small terrier. The head is quite small with a flattish skull and a short muzzle. The nose is black. The dark eyes are medium-sized and have an intelligent, alert expression. The small V-shaped ears are carried erect. The compact body has a level back and is carried on shortish, straight legs. The tail is usually docked to about half its natural length.

Coat Long, straight and glossy with a silky texture; the hair is longer on the head. The main body-color is dark steel-blue, the hair on the head being a rich golden-tan, and that on the chest a bright tan.

Size *Height:* male 8in (20.5cm); female 7in (18cm). *Weight:* 7lb (3kg).

Characteristics and Temperament
Groomed to the peak of perfection for the show ring, it is hard to believe that this dog, with its lustrous, flowing coat and colorful bows in its hair, is also, given half the chance, a typical terrier. This means that it is tough, active and ready for action whenever the opportunity presents itself.

Based on AKC registrations, the Yorkshire Terrier became the second most popular dog breed in the United States in 2006, trailing only a little behind the Labrador Retriever.

INDEX

252

ACKNOWLEDGEMENTS

Front Cover: Flickr Creative Commons/Robert Son of Randy.
Back Cover: Wikimedia Commons/Dan Bennett.

©Animal Photography/Sally Anne Thompson; pages 10, 11, 14 both, 18, 19 right, 24 both, 27 right, 28, 29, 32 both, 34 both, 35, 37 both, 45 both, 46 below, 50 both, 53, 55, 58, 59 below, 60 both, 61, 62 above, 64 below, 65, 67, 71 below, 72 both, 76, 77 below, 78, 79, 80, 84, 86, 87, 88, 89 above, 90, 92, 93 both, 96, 97, 100 above, 101, 104, 105, 106, 107, 108 both, 110 both, 111 top, 112, 113, 114 both, 115, 116 below, 117, 119, 128, 129 both, 130, 132, 133, 134 both, 135, 136 both, 137, 138 below, 139, 142 below, 143, 148, 149, 151 both, 152 below, 153, 155, 157, 159, 160, 161, 165, 168, 173, 176, 177, 179 above, 181, 184, 185, 188, 189, 194, 195, 197, 198 above, 199, 200 both, 201, 202, 203, 204, 205, 206, 207, 208, 209, 211, 213, 216, 217, 219, 220 below, 221, 224, 225, 226 below, 227, 230 both, 231 both, 232, 233, 234, 236, 237 both, 239, 240, 241, 242, 244 above, 245, 246, 247, 249, 250, 251 both. © iStockphoto/Andrea Krause; page 16 left. © iStockphoto/Emmanuelle Bonzami; page 73. © iStockphoto/Jacintha van Beemen. © iStockphoto/Matt Strauss; page 47 below. © iStockphoto/Olga Drozdova; page 95. © Regency House Publishing Ltd.: page 56.

Flickr Creative Commons/: Aaron Anderer; page 163 below. Aislinn Richie; page 144 below. Andrew Villasis; page 131. Andy Armstrong; page 44. Arne List; page 218 above. Beatrice Murch; pages 85, 99 both. Belinda Hawkins Muller; pages 123, 146 below. Ben Lunsford; page 182. Bernt Rostad; page 81. Bob Jagendorf; page 74 above. Cayenne 2006/Nici; pages 40 above, 41. Chadh; page 243 above. Cheneworth; page 218 below. Chris Doelle; page 154. Christopher Walker; pages 6, 121 below. Crista Connelly; page 248 above. Claire73-/yeah it's fixed; page 171 below. Clare Savory; page 31 below right. Dardeche; page 175. Dave Appleby; page 16 right. Dave Merrett; page 31 below left. Dave Poe; page 82. Derek Purdy; page 118 both. Dirk Mueller; page 68 below. Dr. Wendy TL/WTL; page 243 below. Eddie Callaway; page 180 below. Elaine M. Stirling; page 38 below. Eric Ward; page 121 above. FotoDawg; page 94 above. Guido "random" Alvarez; page 220 above. Gunnandreassen; page 66 above. Intangible Arts/Hawkins; page 174. Jason Riedy; page 244 below. Jeffrey Beall; page 223 below. Jennifer Graevell; page 144 above. Joe Hall; page 187. Joe Quercia; page 64 above. John Hurd; pages 190, 191 both. John Leslie; pages 19 left, 146 above, 147. Jon Bennett; page 91. Jsorbieus; page 71 above. Kaitlyn Means; page 127 above. Kamil Porembinski; page 186. Kannonn; page 2. Kathleen Conklin; page 248 below. Kirk Kuenkel; page 57. Lindy Ireland; page 13 left. Liza 31337; page 8. Llima Orosa; page 163 above. Madaise; page 238 both. Marya; page 150 above. Maufdi; pages 38 above, 39 both, 54 both. Maurice Koop; pages 170, 187 above. Mc.Glasgow; page 103. Mike Baird; page 68 above. Mike Bostock; page 83 below. Mike Griggs; page 15 both. Misterjingo; page 228 Mitch D50; page 183. Niko Herlin; pages 12, 13 right. Noel Zia Lee; pages 26, 27 left Owen Byrne; page 127 below. Pato Garzo; page 180 above. Pedro Lopez; pages 74 below, 75. Peter Wadsworth; page 70. Phototram; page 186. Pirate-renee: pages 124 both, 125 below. Psmithy/Peter; page 77 above. Rad Dewey; page 172. Randy Hausken; page 158 both. Randy Son of Robert; pages 120, 142 above. Ron Armstrong; page 145, 222 both. Rover J_P; pages 4, 9, 20 both, 21 ScottKs1; page 162. Scott Robinson; pages 30, 31 above left & right. Shoe the Linux Librarian; page 152 above. Stuart Richards; page 5. Sugar Pond; page 48. SuperFantastic/Bruce; page 83 above. Susie; page 171 above. Tanakawho; pages 126 below, 212. Tanais/tf: pages 122, 141. Thomas Tringale; page 125 above. Tigerzeye/JeffM; page 223 above. Tommy Green; page 150 below. Trent Roche; page 17. Visa Kopu; page 193. Uber Phot; pages 3, 47 above. Van Nuys/Andy; page 126 above. Vox Efx; page 229, 251 above. Winky; pages 42 both, 43. Yola Simon; page 69 both. Zenia; page 156.

Wikimedia Commons/: Wikimedia; page 198 below. Achim Stelter; page 102 above. Amy Lawson; page 22 below. Angela; page 49 left. Beninho; page 214. Bluesik; page 52. Cerie; page 215. Cheesy Mike; page 66 below. Christian Gidlof; page 169. Christian Madden; page 178 below. Christopher Woo; page 62 below. Dan Bennett; page 23 below. Daphne Geerling; page 196 below. Davepaku; page 196 above. D. Lindsay; page 138 above. Dmitry Guskov; page 25 both. Eli Duke; page 140 Faigl.ladislav; page 192 above. Fir0002: page 63. Gemma Longman; page 116 above Helene Gisin; page 109 both. Jay Gorman; page 22 above. Jon Haslam; page 164 Karakal; page 192 below. Lilly M; pages 36 both, 49 right, 89 below Margarita Storahay; page 23 above. Marujen; page 111 below. Pleple 2000; pages 7, 51, 59 above, 98, 179 below, 210, 226 above. Roland Muller-Hagen; page 94 below. Ron Armstrong; pages 46 above, 102 below, 178 above. Sami Kronqvist; page 100 below. Sheri Terris; page 235. Soulkeeper; page 40 below. Staff Sgt. Stacy L. Pearsall; page 166-167.